Taoist Astrology

Taoist Astrology

A HANDBOOK OF THE AUTHENTIC

CHINESE TRADITION

SUSAN LEVITT WITH JEAN TANG

DESTINY BOOKS
ROCHESTER, VERMONT

To the sacredness of animals, that we may love them and learn from them.

Destiny Books
One Park Street
Rochester, Vermont 05767
www.InnerTraditions.com

Destiny Books is a division of Inner Traditions International

LIBRARY OF CONGRESS CATALOGING-IN-PUBLICATION DATA
Levitt, Susan.
    Taoist astrology : a handbook of the authentic Chinese tradition / Susan Levitt with Jean Tang.
        p.   cm.
    Includes bibliographical references and index.
    ISBN 978-089281606-4
    1. Astrology, Taoist. I. Tang, Jean. II. Title.
BF1714.T34L48   1997   97-10330
133.5'949514—dc21   CIP

Printed and bound in the United States

10 9 8

Text design and layout by Kristin Camp
This book was typeset in Weiss with Gill Sans as the display typeface

CONTENTS

ACKNOWLEDGMENTS

Thank you to our youngest sisters, Char Dog and Little Pig, for their love, understanding, and kindness. Gratitude to editor Chuck Gutro, the quintessential Tiger, for his enthusiasm and dedication. Appreciation to three wise men at Destiny Books: green Horse Jon Graham, yellow Monkey Rowan Jacobsen, and gold Ox Ehud Sperling.

What is the greatest fire?
Greed.
What is the greatest crime?
Hatred.
What is the greatest sorrow?
Separation.
The greatest sickness?
Hunger of the heart.
And the greatest joy?
The joy of freedom.
Freedom from desire.
Freedom from possessions.
Freedom from attachment and appetite.
How does one meet suffering?
By pursuing happiness.
Speak and act with a pure heart and mind
and happiness will follow you like a shadow, unshakable.

from *Journey to the West*

ONE

Taoist Astrology

THE WAY OF THE TAO

Everywhere on our planet—from the pyramids of Egypt to the monoliths of Stonehenge in England, to the observatory in the forbidden city of Beijing—ancient people looked up to the night sky. Astrologers observed planetary motion and cycles of the moon and predicted events that paralleled celestial movements.

The ancient Chinese people developed their science of astrology based on their unique spiritual view of the world. The ancient ones studied nature to make sense of the universe. They observed the sky above and the earth below. Through nature they saw growth and decay, death and renewal, strength and life. The complementary structure of the natural order became the religion of Taoism (pronounced "Dowism"). Priests of Taoism, who were both female and male, discovered and developed astronomy, alchemy, geometry, anatomy, herbology, crafts, and animal domestication.

In the distant past, humanity's relationship with animals was necessary for survival. When animals were domesticated, Taoist priests observed the animals' traits. Over the centuries, the priests developed a system of twelve animals for a twelve-year cycle. Human physical and temperamental attributes correlated with certain years. This system became the twelve earthly branches. In the year 2637 B.C., the Chinese Emperor Huang Ti standardized this

Taoist twelve-year calendar, which has been in continuous use ever since.

According to the ancient Taoists, all of life is interconnected. This connection, the Tao, is symbolized by the familiar image known as yin and yang. Traditionally, yin is the dark, feminine, and receptive principle. Yang is the light, masculine, and active principle. Together, yin and yang flow endlessly into each other. Each creates and defines the other's opposite. Without the existence of dark, the concept of light would have no meaning. Similarly, high is defined by low, and sweet is defined by sour.

In western thought, the balance of yin and yang could be seen as conflicting opposites. Yet in Taoist thought there is no such antagonism. Yin is considered the dark side of the mountain. Yang is considered the light side of the mountain. Yet it is still the same mountain.

Even today yin and yang remain the natural order of the universe because the yin and yang cycle repeats endlessly. For example, high noon, the most yang time, progresses to midnight, the most yin hour. Summer solstice, the longest day, is the most yang time of the year. It progresses to winter solstice, the longest night, which is the most yin. Even in our bodies we experience the endless dance of yin and yang. As we inhale our lungs expand to the most yang point, and when we exhale they contract to the most yin point.

Diet and climate are also classified as yin and yang. For example, Native American Inuit people of the polar regions live in a cold yin environment. Their yin weather is balanced by eating a yang diet of raw meat. People living in the hot yang tropics stay healthy by eating a diet of yin fruit.

All of us have both yin and yang qualities—life is a balance of yin and yang. Death occurs when yin and yang separate. Here is a short list of some of the many qualities of the Tao:

Yin	Yang
female	male
moon	sun
water	fire
dark	light
cold	hot
wet	dry
slow	fast
passive	aggressive
receptive	assertive
round	angular
smooth	rough
intuition	intellect
below	above
earth	heaven

The Taoist philosopher Lao-tzu, born in 604 B.C., was the author of the Tao Te Ching, the book of the Tao. Lao-tzu distilled Taoist wisdom into eighty-one short chapters of verse. He understood that we can live in perfect grace, truth, and harmony by accepting the changes of life, just as the natural world acquiesces to the changes in nature. There is no concept of sin, and evil is not condemned. Lao-tzu's view was that a good man was a bad man's teacher, and that teaching a bad man was a good man's responsibility. Lao-tzu explained the harmonious yet dualistic principles of yin and yang:

When some things are deemed beautiful,
other things become ugly.
When things are deemed good,
other things become bad.

Existence and nonexistence create each other.
Difficult and easy produce each other.
Long and short are fashioned from each other.
High and low contrast each other.
Before and behind follow each other.

Taoist culture existed for thousands of years before the first Chinese dynasty (the Shang, circa 1523 to 1027 B.C.). The first dynasty was formed during the Bronze Age when the arts of metallurgy were developed and refined. The ancient Shang people also created a pictographic script with which to express abstract ideas. Archeological discoveries unearthed many inscribed bones that were used for divination, indicating the spiritual and mystical values of the Shang times.

Many centuries later, the religions of Confucianism and Buddhism became part of Chinese culture. Confucianism was based on the teachings of the Chinese scholar Confucius (circa 551 to 479 B.C.). Buddhism came to China from India in the year A.D.68.

About 1027 B.C. the Shangs were overthrown by the Chous, who established their own dynasty. But political trouble and social unrest existed during the end of the Chou dynasty (1028 to 256 B.C.). The Chou empire declined due to warring feudal states within the Chou feudal system. But the Chou dynasty was also a time of great intellectual and artistic ferment. Taoist philosophers from the late Chou period (600 to 222 B.C.) include Lao-tzu and Mo Ti (born circa 500 B.C.), the teacher of universal love. The third great Chou philosopher was K'ung-tzu, or Confucius (circa 551 to 479 B.C.).

Unlike Taoism, Confucianism was based on strict moral laws. Confucian philosophy taught how to govern and emphasized family devotion (filial piety), ancestor worship, and the maintenance of justice and peace. Confucius's sayings and anecdotes about rules of conduct are *Luen-yu* (Confucian Analects). His famous book, *Ou-Shu-Si Jiao*, or Twenty-Four Stories of Filial Devotion, describes how children sacrificed for their parents. These extreme sacrifices parallel Christian stories about saints' martyrdom.

Confucianism was based on five classic books that every nobleman and landowner committed to memory. One of the classics, the I Ching, or Book of Changes, was a fortune-telling system based on Taoist observation of nature and inspired by the patterns of a turtle shell. Confucius himself said in his old age, "If some years could be added to my life, I would give fifty of them to study the

Book of Changes, for then I would have avoided great errors."*

Most ideas of Confucius were counter to Taoism. Lao-tzu felt that simplicity of the heart would lead to balanced manners and rituals. But conservative Confucius felt that humanity needed to be trained and controlled through strict observation of social rules. Many passages of the Tao Te Ching are rebuttals to Confucius's law-and-order morality.

When China became a great empire in the Han dynasty (206 B.C. to A.D. 221) under Emperor Kao Tsu, Confucianism of the late Chou period was restudied and developed. Confucianism then became the court ideology, won the rivalry between it and Taoism, and became the religion of the empire. Strict Confucian laws were politically advantageous to the land-owning class because the tenets of Confucianism supported and modulated the Chinese imperial structure. Confucian laws, not Taoist simplicity, molded the character of China.

After Buddhism came to China in A.D. 68, Buddhist religion quietly coexisted with Taoism and Confucianism. But in the fifth century (the Northern Wei dynasty, A.D. 386 to 535) central Asiatic Tartars from the region of Mongolia took control of northern China. These invaders made Buddhism the official religion in China. Taoism veiled itself in Buddhist doctrine in order to survive. For example, the order of the twelve Taoist zodiac animals was explained as the order in which the animals raced to the bedside of the dying Buddha. Rat came first, followed by Ox. This myth replaced the ancient Taoist folktale whereby clever Rat outwitted Ox to become the first animal (see page 47).

The basis of Buddhist religion was a divine masculine trinity that predates Christianity by thousands of years. This divine trinity was composed of Brahma the creator, Vishnu the preserver, and Shiva the destroyer. Destruction was not necessarily evil. Rather it served a purpose. As one manifestation was destroyed by Shiva, Brahma re-created something new, which was preserved by Vishnu,

*Paul Carus, *Chinese Astrology: Early Chinese Occultism* (Peru, Ill.: Open Court, 1947) 117.

only to be destroyed again by Shiva. This endless cycle of destruction and creation is similar to the Taoist dance of yin and yang.

Chinese Buddhism incorporated Taoist metaphysical concepts and became Chan Buddhism. When Chan Buddhism reached Japan, it incorporated concepts of indigenous Japanese Shinto spirituality and became Zen Buddhism. Like Taoism, Shintoism is based on the cycles of the natural world.

地

支

THE TWELVE EARTHLY BRANCHES

You can determine your earthly branch animal sign by finding your year of birth on the following chart. If you were born in late January or early February, check the lunar calendar that begins each animal chapter in part 2 for your exact birth date. Your earthly branch animal is not determined by the Western New Year that begins on January 1 because the Taoist New Year begins on the second new moon after the winter solstice. The Taoist year begins on a new moon, unlike the Western year that begins January 1 and ends on December 31. For example, if you were born in January 1967 please don't assume you are a Sheep, for the Sheep year began on February 9, 1967. Instead you are a Horse, a very different animal!

Chinese years that include the first day of spring are considered the most favorable. February 2 is the first day of spring, which occurs six weeks after the winter solstice and six weeks before the spring equinox. In the Western calendar February 2 is Groundhog Day, a holiday that harks back to earlier times when the first day of spring was a time of augury derived from the movements of animals. In the old European calendar, this first spring day was the pagan holiday Imbolc, which the Christianizing Romans later renamed Candlemas.

The Taoist lunar year often includes the first day of spring. It occurs either in the beginning or the end of the year. A year that includes the first day of spring is considered extremely favorable for marriage, having children, buying property, and starting or expanding a business. A year without a first day of spring is not favorable and is considered a "blind" year because the first day of spring was not seen. Therefore, unforeseen complications may develop.

The lunar calendar of Taoist astrology is used all over Asia. Chinese, Japanese, and Korean astrology are patterned after Taoist astrology, and the terms are used interchangeably.

THE TWELVE EARTHLY BRANCHES

Rat: 1900, 1912, 1924, 1936, 1948, 1960, 1972, 1984, 1996, 2008

Ox: 1901, 1913, 1925, 1937, 1949, 1961, 1973, 1985, 1997, 2009

Tiger: 1902, 1914, 1926, 1938, 1950, 1962, 1974, 1986, 1998, 2010

Hare: 1903, 1915, 1927, 1939, 1951, 1963, 1975, 1987, 1999, 2011

Dragon: 1904, 1916, 1928, 1940, 1952, 1964, 1976, 1988, 2000, 2012

Serpent: 1905, 1917, 1929, 1941, 1953, 1965, 1977, 1989, 2001, 2013

Horse: 1906, 1918, 1930, 1942, 1954, 1966, 1978, 1990, 2002, 2014

Sheep: 1907, 1919, 1931, 1943, 1955, 1967, 1979, 1991, 2003, 2015

Monkey: 1908, 1920, 1932, 1944, 1956, 1968, 1980, 1992, 2004, 2016

Phoenix: 1909, 1921, 1933, 1945, 1957, 1969, 1981, 1993, 2005, 2017

Dog: 1910, 1922, 1934, 1946, 1958, 1970, 1982, 1994, 2006, 2018

Boar: 1911, 1923, 1935, 1947, 1959, 1971, 1983, 1995, 2007, 2019

The animals of the twelve earthly branches are determined by seasonal cycles:

Rat is the first earthly branch and the seed, the start of a cycle. It is the beginning of the winter season. The ability to be first in all things is a Rat trait. The first earthly branch represents

December, the eleventh month in the Taoist lunar calendar. December is the time of Sagittarius, Rat's Western counterpart.

Ox is the second earthly branch. This phase represents the beginning stages of a plant's growth, the seed's struggle to break out of confinement and sprout. This determination and perseverance in struggle are Ox qualities. The second earthly branch represents January, the twelfth lunar month. January is the time of Capricorn, Ox's Western counterpart.

Tiger is the third earthly branch. This phase is symbolized by the vigilant new sprout that has just broken free from the earth. People born in a Tiger year share the same positive and upward-reaching qualities as a growing sprout. The third earthly branch represents February, the first lunar month. February is the time of Aquarius, Tiger's Western counterpart.

Hare is the fourth earthly branch. This phase is the beginning of spring. It symbolizes the effortless growth of plants in warm, magical spring light. The gentle qualities of springtime are traits of those born in Hare year. The fourth earthly branch represents March, the second lunar month. March is the time of Pisces, Hare's Western counterpart.

Dragon is the fifth earthly branch. This phase happens when plants are growing and vigorously expanding. The life force, the yang part of the universe, is very strong. This powerful life force is fully visible in people who are born in the year of the Dragon. The fifth earthly branch represents April, the third lunar month. April is the time of Aries, Dragon's Western counterpart.

Serpent is the sixth earthly branch. During this phase, plants have completed their growth. This turning point brings the outward growth inward, turning vigor and power into wisdom. These characteristics are reflected in people born in the year of the Serpent. The sixth earthly branch symbolizes May, the fourth lunar month. May is the time of Taurus, Serpent's Western counterpart.

Horse is the seventh earthly branch. This phase occurs when the sun is brightest and the plants are strong, having reached maturity. Horse people possess a sunny disposition and are bright, open, and cheerful. The seventh earthly branch symbolizes June, the fifth lunar month. June is the time of Gemini, Horse's Western counterpart.

Sheep is the eighth earthly branch. It is the phase when plants are ripening and all is peaceful. This gentle peacefulness is the core of Sheep's nature. The eighth earthly branch symbolizes July, the sixth lunar month. July is the time of Cancer, Sheep's Western counterpart.

Monkey is the ninth earthly branch. During this phase, crops are ready to harvest. That is why Monkeys naturally have so many developed talents and abilities. The ninth branch symbolizes August, the seventh lunar month. August is the time of Leo, Monkey's Western counterpart.

Phoenix is the tenth earthly branch. This phase occurs during the month of harvest and prosperity. Responsibility, duty, and satisfaction for work well done characterize people born in the year of the Phoenix. The tenth earthly branch symbolizes September, the eighth lunar month. September is the time of Virgo, Phoenix's Western counterpart.

Dog is the eleventh earthly branch. During this phase plants gradually disintegrate and return to Mother Earth while the animals prepare for winter. This ability to diligently prepare and be responsible are qualities of those born in the year of the Dog. The eleventh earthly branch symbolizes October, the ninth lunar month. October is the time of Libra, Dog's Western counterpart.

Boar is the twelfth earthly branch. This is the phase when earth is at rest in winter, and a sense of peacefulness is prevalent. Love of rest and cultivation of peace are Boar qualities. The twelfth earthly branch symbolizes November, the tenth lunar month. November is the time of Scorpio, Boar's Western counterpart.

The Taoists consider six signs—Rat, Tiger, Dragon, Horse, Monkey, and Dog—to be yang and the other six signs—Ox, Hare, Serpent, Sheep, Phoenix, and Boar—to be yin. Since traditionally yang is associated with masculine forces and yin with feminine ones, in this book for readability we refer to the yang signs as "he" and the yin signs as "she." We trust that no one will be dismayed by having to read a pronoun that does not refer to her or his gender.

The twelve earthly branches are embellished with animal folktales that have been handed down in the oral tradition for many generations. Even the simplest person could learn by listening to the myriad folktales about animals.

Many animals are considered sacred in Asia, not just the twelve animals of the Taoist zodiac. Other sacred animals are represented under a similar animal sign. For examples, the proud and strong lion possesses the attributes of Tiger. The beloved cat shares the attributes of Hare. The ancient turtle appears in other Taoist works, such as the divination system of the I Ching and the art of feng-shui (pronounced "fung shway"), a system of Taoist geomancy. Other animals, such as praying mantis, bear, deer, and crane, are represented in the Taoist martial arts.

YOUR RISING SIGN

When people meet you, they see how you look, act, and react. How you appear to others, their first impression, is determined by your rising sign. It is your personal expression and style that others identify, notice, and superficially comprehend. The rising sign also influences your physical appearance and how you accomplish your daily affairs. It is your attitude about how you approach life tasks.

In Western astrology, the rising sign (also known as the ascendant) is the sign appearing at the horizon during your birth. But the Taoist rising sign is determined by the hour you were born. Your rising-sign animal is second to your birth-year animal. Still, it flavors personality and shapes character. This is especially true of those born in a gentle animal year (such as Hare, Sheep, or Boar) who have power animals as rising signs (such as Tiger, Dragon, Serpent, or Monkey).

Relationship compatibility is enhanced with harmonious rising-sign animals or a rising-sign animal that compliments a birth-year animal. In determining compatibility, study the relationship between both the birth-year animals and the rising-sign animals. For example, Dog is not usually compatible with Dragon. But a Dog with Monkey rising can be compatible with Dragon because Monkey and Dragon are very harmonious together. Even if your birth-year animal is not harmonious with that of another person, your rising signs may be compatible, which will bring ease to your interactions.

The following chart indicates your rising sign:

11 P.M. to 1 A.M.—Hours ruled by Rat. Rat qualities are a quick mind, a good bargainer, and a natural charmer. This influence gives the foresight to plan, invest wisely, and not be confused or duped by others.

1 A.M. to 3 A.M.—Hours ruled by Ox. Ox qualities are steadiness, perseverance, and determination. This influence gives the strength to work hard, value family, and accomplish for the common good.

3 A.M. to 5 A.M.—Hours ruled by Tiger. Tiger qualities are vigor, leadership, and courage. This influence gives the talent to dazzle, have many friends, and relate well to different types of people.

5 A.M. to 7 A.M.—Hours ruled by Hare. Hare qualities are friendliness, diplomacy, and adaptability. This influence gives the grace to be kind, gentle, and soft-spoken.

7 A.M. to 9 A.M.—Hours ruled by Dragon. Dragon qualities are power, passion, and drive. This influence adds intensity to life and drama and excitement in relationships, and it can also bring opportunities for travel.

9 A.M. to 11 A.M.—Hours ruled by Serpent. Serpent qualities are wisdom, mystery, and sensuality. This influence brings the gifts of patience, intuition, and understanding of the human psyche.

11 A.M. to 1 P.M.—Hours ruled by Horse. Horse qualities are good humor, friendliness, and a carefree attitude. This influence gives the joy to be popular and well liked, an adventuresome spirit, and a dash of daring.

1 P.M. to 3 P.M.—Hours ruled by Sheep. Sheep qualities are gentleness, compassion, and love of the good life. This influence brings an artistic, inventively creative, and peaceful overtone to the personality.

3 P.M. to 5 P.M.—Hours ruled by Monkey. Monkey qualities are a quick wit, many talents, and lack of inhibition. This influence enables one to succeed at a variety of occupations, get the best

deal, and be witty or charming.

5 P.M. to 7 P.M.—Hours ruled by Phoenix. Phoenix qualities are keen judgment, good planning, and sharp perception. This influence brings the ability to handle money well, be skeptical or suspicious when necessary, and to work hard to achieve success.

7 P.M. to 9 P.M.—Hours ruled by Dog. Dog qualities are honesty, idealism, and unselfishness. This influence gives the ability to be a true friend, a trusted soul, and guided by high moral principles.

9 P.M. to 11 P.M.—Hours ruled by Boar. Boar qualities are a peaceful nature, optimism, and sensitivity. This influence brings the knack to enjoy life, easily share with others, and find contentment.

If you are born right on the hour when the rising sign changes, you may experience the influences of both signs. But the yang animal's influence will take precedence over the yin animal's influence.

Some combinations of birth-year animal and rising-sign animal may seem less compatible than other combinations. For example, a Hare with Phoenix rising may experience conflict concerning whether to honor the gentle, noncompetitive Hare nature or to develop the perfectionist, success-oriented Phoenix nature. Cultivate your signs' natural talents regardless of your gender! A female Monkey with Dragon rising can successfully express her strong energy as a dynamic powerhouse who runs her own business. A male Hare with Sheep rising can find peace as an artistic gardener who specializes in flowering herbs.

One can blend seeming incompatible animal qualities by integrating all aspects into one's character. Lao-tzu's wisdom in the Tao Te Ching explains:

> *Know the strength of the male*
> *yet keep the female's care.*
> *Know the white*
> *yet keep to the black.*
> *Know honorable action*
> *yet stay humble.*

五天
行干

FIVE ELEMENTS AND
TEN HEAVENLY STEMS

The twelve branches of Taoist astrology are structured on five elements: fire, earth, metal, water, and wood. The five Taoist elements also can be translated as the five powers, virtues, phases, or changing elements. The ancient Taoists created the five elements as distinct energies. These energies are always moving, unstable and changeable, like the dance of yin and yang. Everything on earth and in heaven is characterized by the constant interplay between the five elements.

Although the Taoist concept of yin and yang is many millennia old, the five elements were not documented until the fourth century B.C. The late Chou period (600 to 222 B.C.) was a time of philosophical upheaval (see page 5) during which the five element theory was developed and studied. The five elements were systematized by the Chinese scholar Zou Yen (circa 350 to 270 B.C.). Later, the five elements were popularized throughout China during the Sung dynasty (A.D. 960 to 1279).

Even in modern times, knowledge of the five elements remains important to character development, self-knowledge, and health, as does knowledge of your personal Taoist animal.

The five elements exist in either a yin or yang state. These five elements in their yin or yang manifestation are the ten heavenly stems. Each stem is assigned a color depending on its element and gender, with yang being "masculine" and yin being "feminine."

This is how color is assigned to each of the twelve animals. Your Taoist element and color are determined by the last number of your birth year. (This may not apply to those born in late January or early February because the Taoist year begins after January 1. See page 8.)

Six earthly branches are yang, "masculine," and active: Rat, Tiger, Dragon, Horse, Monkey, and Dog. For example, metal Rat is white because Rat is yang. Yang years end in even numbers.

Six earthly branches are yin, "feminine," and receptive: Ox, Hare, Serpent, Sheep, Phoenix, and Boar. For example, metal Ox is silver because Ox is yin. Yin years end in odd numbers.

Metal years end in zero and one. Yang metal is white. Yin metal is silver.

    White years end in zero: 1900, 1910, 1920, 1930, 1940, 1950, 1960, 1970, 1980, 1990, 2000, 2010, etc.

    Silver years end in number one: 1901, 1911, 1921, 1931, 1941, 1951, 1961, 1971, 1981, 1991, 2001, 2011, etc.

Water years end in numbers two and three. Yang water is black. Yin water is gray.

    Black years end in number two: 1902, 1912, 1922, 1932, 1942, 1952, 1962, 1972, 1982, 1992, 2002, 2012, etc.

    Gray years end in number three: 1903, 1913, 1923, 1933, 1943, 1953, 1963, 1973, 1983, 1993, 2003, 2013, etc.

Wood years end in numbers four and five. Yang wood is green. Yin wood is blue.

    Green years end in number four: 1904, 1914, 1924, 1934, 1944, 1954, 1964, 1974, 1984, 1994, 2004, 2014, etc.

    Blue years end in number five: 1905, 1915, 1925, 1935, 1945, 1955, 1965, 1975, 1985, 1995, 2005, 2015, etc.

Fire years end in numbers six and seven. Yang fire is red. Yin fire is purple.

    Red years end in number six: 1906, 1916, 1926, 1936, 1946, 1956, 1966, 1976, 1986, 1996, 2006, 2016, etc.

    Purple years end in number seven: 1907, 1917, 1927, 1937, 1947, 1957, 1967, 1977, 1987, 1997, 2007, 2017, etc.

Earth years end in numbers eight and nine. Yang earth is yellow.
 Yin earth is gold.
  Yellow years end in number eight: 1908, 1918, 1928, 1938, 1948,
   1958, 1968, 1978, 1988, 1998, 2008, 2018, etc.
  Gold years end in number nine: 1909, 1919, 1929, 1939, 1949,
   1959, 1969, 1979, 1989, 1999, 2009, 2019, etc.

The combination of the twelve branches, and the five elements in
their yin and yang states, results in a never-ending history of sixty-
year cycles. Each sixty-year cycle begins during a fire Rat year.
The most recent sixty-year cycle started on the new moon of February 19, 1996 (the year 4694 in the Chinese calendar).

火 FIRE

Each element possesses distinct characteristics. The first element,
fire, is the most masculine of the five elements. Therefore, it is
considered very yang. Fire's planet is Mars, the intense red planet.
Fire's season is summer, the time of heat, growth, warmth, and
increased light. Fire corresponds to the three earthly branches of
summertime: Serpent (May), Horse (June), and Sheep (July). Fire's
direction is south.

Although fire is considered a very yang element in general, it
can exist in either a yang or a yin state, because in Taoism all things
have both a yin and a yang expression to create balance. Brilliant,
life-giving sunlight is an example of fire in its yang state, while
romantic, mysterious candlelight is an example of this yang element at its most yin extreme. When fire expresses masculine yang
energy, its color is red and is symbolized by burning wood. When
fire expresses feminine yin energy, its color is purple and is symbolized by the flame of a lamp.

Fire personality traits are love, passion, leadership, spirituality,
insight, dynamism, aggression, intuition, reason, and expressiveness. The fire personality is direct—right out front. A fire type

---

FIRE
Colors: red (yang) and purple (yin)
Earthly branches and months: Serpent (May), Horse (June),
    Sheep (July)
Planet: Mars
Direction: south
Climate: hot
Season: summer
Emotion: happiness
Body organs: heart (yin) and small intestines (yang)

---

succeeds by becoming warmhearted and generous. Experiences of love, compassion, fun, joy, and pleasure are healing for fire individuals. The challenge for a fire type is to share joy and laughter without thought of reward.

The emotion associated with fire is happiness. Other fire emotions include joy, vanity, jealousy, frustration, regret, grief from loss of love, and disappointment in relationships. A red or purple sign must not indulge in the unpleasant personality trait of excessive arrogance.

In Taoist medicine, fire's body organs are the heart and small intestines. Therefore red or purple signs may have a disposition for heart problems, such as heart attacks, or may experience minor digestive problems in the small intestines. A red sign is extremely resilient and can miraculously overcome most illnesses. A purple sign may have a disposition to develop a weak heart due to emotional stress. The element wood nurtures the element fire; wood's body organ is the liver. Red or purple signs must avoid alcoholic beverages that heat (overstimulate) the liver. Liver excess is a false way to empower the heart and causes imbalance between fire and wood. Heart illness and fire imbalance can often be read in the face: a cleft in the nose or an overly red complexion.

土 EARTH

The element earth is yin, feminine, like Mother Earth in the West. Earth's planet is Saturn. Earth corresponds to all twelve earthly branches, and its "season" is the last eighteen days of each of the four seasons, the time of seasonal transition. Earth's location (direction) is the center.

Although earth is a yin element, it can exist in either a yang or a yin state. When earth expresses masculine yang energy, its color is yellow and is symbolized by a hill. When earth expresses feminine yin energy, its color is gold and is symbolized by a valley. People born in a golden year are considered fortunate and will always be taken care of and have their needs met.

Earth personalities are stable, practical, reliable, industrious, empathetic, honest, kind, prudent. Earth types value friendship. An earth individual does well to meditate and contemplate. It is important for those born in an earth year to nourish themselves physically, emotionally, and spiritually. They must learn to develop clear boundaries and take care of themselves. The challenge for earth types is to honor their sympathetic nature and show great kindness to others.

The emotion associated with earth is sympathy. Other earth

EARTH

Colors: yellow (yang) and gold (yin)

Earthly branches and months: All twelve branches are earthly. No months are earthly.

Planet: Saturn

Direction: center

Climate: damp

Season: seasonal transition—the last eighteen days of the four seasons

Emotion: sympathy

Body organs: stomach (yang) and spleen (yin)

---

qualities are pensiveness, thoughtfulness, and reflection. Just as one assimilates nutrients through the stomach, one assimilates life experiences through the element earth. A strong earth element helps one to digest and accept fate and expand one's circle of knowledge.

In Taoist medicine, earth's body organs are the stomach and spleen. Yellow or gold signs should avoid foods that antagonize the stomach because they may have a disposition for stomach disorders, such as ulcers or indigestion. A weak spleen can cause immune system problems due to poor assimilation of nutrients. Since the sweet taste is associated with the element earth, yellow or gold signs could develop a sweet tooth. They must avoid the tendency to indulge in too many sweets and rich desserts. Stomach illness and earth imbalance are indicated as deep sagging facial lines from the base of the nose to the outer corners of the lip.

金 METAL

Metal is feminine because it is extracted from the feminine earth, although metal is considered less feminine than earth or water. Metal's planet is Venus. Metal's season is autumn, the time of harvest (with a metal scythe), completion, and the beginning of rest. Metal corresponds to the three earthly branches of fall: Monkey (August), Phoenix (September), and Dog (October). Metal's direction is west.

Although metal is a lesser yin element, it can exist in either a yang or a yin state. When metal expresses masculine yang energy, its color is white and is symbolized by a weapon. When metal expresses feminine yin energy, its color is silver and is symbolized by a kettle.

Metal qualities include strength, independence, focus, intensity, righteousness, and fluency in speech. The metal personality is very determined and powerful. One born in a metal year succeeds by being less opinionated, accepting change, and gracefully releasing the past.

METAL

Colors: white (yang) and silver (yin)

Earthly branches and months: Monkey (August), Phoenix (September), Dog (October)

Planet: Venus

Direction: west

Climate: dry

Season: autumn

Emotion: grief

Body organs: lungs (yin) and large intestines (yang)

The emotion associated with metal is grief. Other metal emotions are insecurity, inability to achieve parental or spousal expectations, and lack of confidence. The challenge for a metal type is to learn how to express grief and find healing.

In Taoist medicine, metal's body organs are the lungs and large intestines. White or silver signs must take care of their lungs for they may be susceptible to colds, cough, flu, pneumonia, tuberculosis, and other respiratory problems. Cigarette smoking is extremely harmful for metal signs. White or silver signs could also develop intestinal problems that result in constipation or poor bowel function. Intestinal and bowel cleansings are helpful for maintaining proper balance.

A sunken chest or labored breathing are signs of weak metal. Also, lung illness and metal imbalance may result in a pale, sickly complexion.

水 WATER

Water is the most feminine of the five elements and therefore is considered very yin. In the Taoist system, femininity is not considered weak. On the contrary, water is the most powerful element for it can move around any obstacle in its path without losing its essential nature. Water can, in time, dissolve the hardest mountains.

WATER
Colors: black (yang) and gray (yin)
Earthly branches and months: Boar (November), Rat (December), Ox (January)
Planet: Mercury
Direction: north
Climate: cold
Season: winter
Emotion: fear
Body organs: kidneys (yin) and bladder (yang)

Water's planet is Mercury. The metal Mercury exists in a liquid form, like water. Water's season is winter and therefore corresponds to the three earthly branches of wintertime: Boar (November), Rat (December), and Ox (January). Water's direction is north.

Although water is a very yin element, it can exist in either a yang or a yin state. When water expresses masculine yang energy, its color is black and is symbolized by a wave. When water expresses feminine yin energy, its color is gray and is symbolized by a brook.

Water qualities are creativity, sensitivity, reflection, persuasion, effectiveness, and desire for life and sex. Water types value family and social contacts and possess the ability to attract (being receptive, water can attract, rather than pursue). The emotion associated with water is fear. Other water emotions are indecisiveness, vacillation, and uncertainty. Those born in a water year succeed by not allowing fear to block the fullest expression of creativity. The challenge for water types is to overcome their fears and become active participants in life.

In Taoist medicine, water's body organs are the kidneys and bladder. Black or gray signs may have a disposition for urinary problems, bladder infections in women, or prostate difficulties in men. Coffee drinking weakens the kidneys, and cocaine abuse causes irreversible kidney damage. These toxic substances, including alcohol and other drugs, must be avoided.

Kidney illness and water imbalance are indicated as dark circles or swollen bags under the eyes. Baldness is often another sign of weak water.

木 WOOD

The element wood is masculine and considered less yang than fire. Wood's planet is Jupiter, the largest planet, symbolic of wood's growth in springtime. Wood's season is spring, the time of planting seeds, beginnings, and new growth. Wood corresponds to the three earthly branches of springtime: Tiger (February), Hare (March), and Dragon (April). Wood's direction is east.

Although wood is a less yang element, it can exist in either a yang or a yin state. When wood expresses masculine yang energy, its color is green and is symbolized by a pine tree—sturdy, upright, and enduring. When wood expresses feminine yin energy, its color is blue and is symbolized by the flexible bamboo that gently bends with the wind.

Wood qualities are bold actions, planning, initiating new projects, idealism, imagination, compassion, and competition. Wood types possess decision-making skills and the ability to create change. From an Asian perspective, the go-getter, do-or-die, pioneering spirit of American culture is very wood. The challenge for a wood type is to learn to control anger and channel it into positive work that benefits all people.

The emotion associated with wood is anger. Other wood emotions are tension, criticism, discouragement, regret, excitement, dislike of self and others, negative judgment, and repressed anger related to thwarted affection.

In Taoist medicine, wood's body organs are the liver and gallbladder. Drinking alcohol is like drinking poison for green and blue signs because alcoholic beverages heat (overstimulate) the liver and cause severe wood imbalance. Avoid greasy, fatty foods that antagonize the gallbladder.

Liver illness and wood imbalance are indicated as furrowed

lines at the brow. A single deep furrow between the brows indicates spleen imbalance and correlates to the element earth.

Wood
Colors: green (yang) and blue (yin)
Earthly branches and months: Tiger (February), Hare (March), Dragon (April)
Planet: Jupiter
Direction: east
Climate: windy
Season: spring
Emotion: anger
Body organs: liver (yin) and gallbladder (yang)

Taoist Alchemy

The alchemical blend of the five Taoist elements creates many healing modalities, including harmonious relationships and compatibility. This is demonstrated in nurturing relationships and friendships. Yet some elemental blends are not harmonious. This is demonstrated in relationships of dependence and conflict. To determine element compatibility, read across the following chart:

Your Element	Your Nurturer	Your Friend	You have No Conflict	You Nurture	You have Conflict
Fire	Wood	Metal	Fire	Earth	Water
Earth	Fire	Water	Earth	Metal	Wood
Metal	Earth	Wood	Metal	Water	Fire
Water	Metal	Fire	Water	Wood	Earth
Wood	Water	Earth	Wood	Fire	Metal

The basic pattern of Taoist elemental compatibility is:

Fire is the parent of earth and the child of wood.
Earth is the parent of metal and the child of fire.
Metal is the parent of water and the child of earth.
Water is the parent of wood and the child of metal.
Wood is the parent of fire and the child of water.

It is comfortable to be with companions who are parental nurturers or friends, or who present no conflict, although marriage to someone sharing your same element is not recommended. But it may be challenging to be with companions you nurture (your child) or conflict with. The following circle depicts the cycle of nurturing.

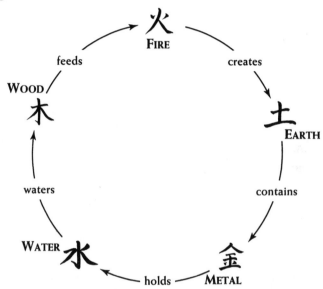

Fire nurtures earth because after fire burns, ashes remain that create more earth crust. Red and purple (fire) are stimulating and invigorating colors for sluggish earth types.

Earth nurtures metal because metal ores are mined from deep within the earth. Yellow and gold (earth) are empowering and healing colors for confused metal types.

Metal nurtures water because water is contained and carried in metal vessels. White and silver (metal) are clear and purifying colors for insecure water types.

Water nurtures wood because watering wood (trees) helps them grow. Black and dark gray (water) are sedating and peaceful colors for wrathful wood types.

Wood nurtures fire because feeding wooden logs to a fire creates a brighter blaze. Green and blue (wood) are calming and soothing colors for overexcited fire types.

The following circle explains the cycle of conflict and control.

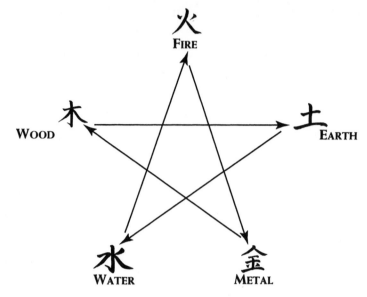

Fire melts metal, which weakens metal. Therefore, one born in a metal year may struggle for power with one born in a fire year.

Earth blocks water, as in dams or dikes, restricting water's flow. Therefore, one born in a water year may be blocked by one born in an earth year.

Metal axes cut wood, which kills wood. Therefore, one born in a wood year could be hurt by one born in a metal year.

Water puts out fire, completely extinguishing fire. Therefore, one born in a fire year could be restricted by one born in a water year.

Wood extracts nutrients from earth to grow, which depletes earth. Therefore, one born in an earth year may be hindered by one born in a wood year.

FIRE COMPATIBILITY FOR RED AND PURPLE SIGNS

Fire with Fire: A red sign is basically harmonious with another red sign because two yang fire signs share similar drive and zeal (born during years ending in number six). They benefit if they work as a team and avoid competition. A red sign may be compatible with a purple sign (born during years ending in number seven), the yin balance to red, because they compliment each other and respond in similar manner. Two purple signs are compatible with each other, for two yin fire signs attain similar goals and share successful strategies.

Fire with Earth: A red or purple sign may not be compatible with a yellow or gold earth sign (born during years ending in number eight or nine) because earth sprinkled over a fire diminishes it. Although fire is helpful to earth because fire is earth's parent, few red or purple fire signs volunteer to give without receiving, especially the red signs.

Fire with Metal: A red or purple sign can be happy when paired with a white or silver metal color (born during years ending with zero or one) who is a good friend and helper. But care must be taken because fire can melt metal. If a red or purple sign overpowers a white and silver sign, the metal type becomes overwhelmed or victimized. In particular, a red sign should avoid direct conflict with any white sign, for metal can retaliate with a vengeance.

Fire with Water: A red or purple sign often experiences difficulty with a black or gray water sign (born during years ending in number two or three). Since water extinguishes fire, signs that are black or gray may hinder or block red or purple signs' progress, even to the point of destruction.

Fire with Wood: A red or purple sign is pleased and content with a green or blue wood sign who is a parental helper, nurturer, and teacher (born during years ending in number four or five). Adding wood makes a fire burn brighter; therefore a green or blue sign can assist a fire sign in achieving goals. But red or purple signs should not use or devour green or blue signs whereby because the wood type may feel depleted or taken advantage of.

EARTH COMPATIBILITY FOR YELLOW AND GOLD SIGNS

Earth with Fire: A yellow or gold sign can be content with a red or purple fire color who is a parental nurturer and helper (born during years ending in number six or seven). Earth is fire's child in that after fire burns it creates ash, making more earth. But yellow or gold signs should be careful and not demand that fire signs burn themselves out while helping.

Earth with Earth: Two yellow signs may be harmonious together, for two yang earth signs share similar values and ideals (born during years ending in number eight). They benefit if they work as a team and avoid competition. A yellow sign is harmonious with a gold sign, its yin equivalent (born during years ending in number nine). They compliment each other and respond in similar manner. Two gold signs are very compatible together, for two yin earth signs share similar values and apply similar methodology to problem solving.

Earth with Metal: A yellow or gold sign may not be happy with a white or silver metal sign (born during years ending in zero or one). Metal is extracted from the earth (earth's child), which upsets earth's balance. The stable earth sign doesn't like disruptions. A yellow or gold sign is helpful to metal, but few earth signs would voluntarily enter a challenging situation.

Earth with Water: A yellow or gold sign can be happy when paired with a black or gray sign (born during years ending in two or three) who is yellow and gold sign's good friend and helper. But earth can block water, just as a dam, dike, or canal holds back water's flow. Therefore, a yellow or gold sign should not overwhelm or tax black or gray companions.

Earth with Wood: Challenging relationships for a yellow or gold sign exist with a green or blue wood sign (born during years ending in number four or five). Since roots of large trees (wood) extract nutrients from earth, a green or blue sign may strain or hinder a yellow or gold sign's progress by being too needy or demanding.

Metal Compatibility for White and Silver Signs

Metal with Fire: A white or silver sign may find problems with a red or purple sign (born during years ending in number six or seven). Difficulties and rivalries easily develop among these opinionated personalities. Fire melts metal; therefore a fire sign may deplete a metal sign.

Metal with Earth: A white or silver sign may be content with a yellow or gold sign who is a parental helper and nurturer (born during years ending in number eight or nine). Since metal is extracted from the earth, an earth sign has much to give. But a white or silver sign should be appreciative of, not just wanting more from, an earth-sign companion.

Metal with Metal: Two white signs can be harmonious together, for two yang metal signs share similar goals and ambitions (born during years ending in zero). They benefit if they work as a team and avoid competition and dishonesty. A white sign may be compatible with a silver sign, the yin balance to white (born during years ending in number one). They compliment each other and respond in similar manner. Two silver signs are harmonious, for two yin metal signs understand each other and respect each other's goals.

Metal with Water: A white or silver sign may not be happy with a black or gray sign (born during years ending in number two or three). A metal container carries water because water is metal's child. But the independent white or silver sign has no desire to carry or take care of anyone else. A metal sign may find a water sign too emotional and needy in relationship.

Metal with Wood: A white or silver sign can be happy when paired with a green or blue wood color, who is a good friend and helper (born during years ending in number four or five). But a white or silver sign must not be cruel or harsh to a wood-sign friend, for a metal ax can cut wood. This applies especially to white signs.

Water Compatibility for Black and Gray Signs

Water with Fire: A black or gray sign can be content with a red or purple fire color, who is a good friend and helper (born during years ending in number six or seven). But water puts out fire, so a black or gray sign should not try to dominate fire-sign friends, especially a black sign who may have an agenda.

Water with Earth: A black or gray sign may experience difficulties with a yellow or gold sign (born during years ending in number eight or nine). Just as an earth dam blocks the flow of water, so can earth signs block the life energy of a black or gray sign.

Water with Metal: A black or gray sign can be happy when paired with a white or gray sign, who is a parental helper and nurturer (born during years ending in zero or one). But a black or gray sign must not take advantage of a metal sign's capacity to give enthusiastically.

Water with Water: Two black signs are harmonious together, for two yang water signs possess similar focus (born during years ending in number two). They benefit if they can work as a team and avoid competition and fighting. A black sign could be fine with a gray sign, the yin balance to black (born during years ending in number three). They compliment each other and respond in similar manner. Two gray signs are harmonious, for two yin water types are sympathetic to each other's difficulties and can be very adept at problem solving for each other.

Water with Wood: A black or gray sign may not be happy with a green or blue wood sign (born during years ending in number four or five). Since wood (trees) benefit when watered, a black or gray sign must do the giving, since wood is water's child. A water sign does not want obligations, and a driven wood sign can be difficult when demanding assistance to achieve a goal.

Wood Compatibility for Green and Blue Signs

Wood with Fire: A green or blue sign may not be harmonious with a red or purple fire sign because fire burns wood (born during years ending in number six or seven). A childish fire sign may demand too much of a parental green or blue sign, who has no desire to live up to anyone else's expectations.

Wood with Earth: A green or blue sign can be content with a yellow or gold earth sign (born during years ending in number eight or nine). Wood (trees) grows out of the earth, so a green or blue sign must not be too demanding of earth types.

Wood with Metal: A green or blue sign may experience chaos with a difficult white or silver metal sign, for a metal ax cuts wood (born during years ending in zero or one). A green or blue sign does not want to be thwarted and does well to avoid a metal sign.

Wood with Water: A green or blue sign can be happy when paired with a black or gray sign, parental helper and nurturer (born during years ending in number two or three). Since water helps wood (trees) grow, a green or blue sign must not be too thirsty or needy with water-sign companions.

Wood with Wood: Two green signs can be harmonious together, for two yang wood signs share similar drive and creativity (born during years ending in number four). They could benefit if they work as a team and avoid competition. A green sign could be fine with blue, the yin balance to green (born during years ending in number five). They compliment each other and respond in similar manner. Together, two blue yin wood signs are compatible and enjoy similar values and a life of contentment.

BALANCING THE FIVE ELEMENTS

The five elements' nurturing and controlling principles are the basis of Taoist medicine. Balanced interaction of these elements brings physical harmony and good health. In Taoist healing, one element cannot exist in isolation from the other elements, although one element may be more imbalanced or diseased and require immediate attention. Consultation with a practitioner of Taoist medicine (traditional Chinese medicine) can determine your body's elemental balances. Acupuncture can help correct body organ imbalances by controlling excessive body organs and nurturing depleted body organs. A holistic medical approach is necessary to create healing because the five elements are in a constant state of movement, change, and flux, like the dance of yin and yang.

For example, fire is associated with the heart. A heart attack results from too much tension (wood) and grief (metal). Both the nurturing and controlling cycles are imbalanced. Fire did not receive nurturing from wood, and fire has excessive control over metal. Another example is that water is associated with the kidneys. Water is nurtured by metal (lungs). The lungs are a respiratory filtering station just as the kidneys are a fluid filtering station. Water is controlled by earth (stomach). Water imbalance from stomach fluids and kidney fluids calcify to create kidney stones.

The elements of fire, water, and earth possess similar qualities in both Western and Taoist astrological systems. The Western element air correlates to Taoist metal, since metal's body organ is the lungs in Taoist medicine and our lungs hold air. Wood is left without a role. But the Taoist system includes wood as a less yang form of fire. Fire is great yang, and wood is lesser yang. For example, great yang is a temperature of one hundred degrees, whereas lesser yang is a temperature of seventy degrees. Likewise, water is great yin, and metal is less yin. A day well below freezing is an example of great yin; less yin is a brisk, cool day. Earth is the center, in complete yin and yang balance.

The Taoist four directions are symbolized by four mythological animals. South's symbol is a red Phoenix. West's symbol is a white Tiger. North's symbol is a black Tortoise. East's symbol is a turquoise Dragon. Sometimes all four directions are symbolized by colored Tigers.

The use of herbal remedies is another integral part of Taoist healing. In the year 3494 B.C. the Chinese Emperor Shen Nong oversaw the development of medicinal remedies derived from plants, animal parts, insects, sea shells, and minerals. Taoist medicine was highly developed in the Han dynasty from careful observation of life cycles. A Han dynasty Taoist folktale tells of a farmer

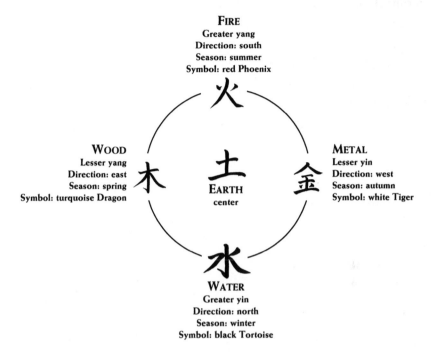

FIRE
Greater yang
Direction: south
Season: summer
Symbol: red Phoenix

火

WOOD
Lesser yang
Direction: east
Season: spring
Symbol: turquoise Dragon

木

土
EARTH
center

METAL
Lesser yin
Direction: west
Season: autumn
Symbol: white Tiger

金

水

WATER
Greater yin
Direction: north
Season: winter
Symbol: black Tortoise

Note: South is always at the top of the Chinese compass

who bludgeoned a serpent with his hoe. The wounded creature managed to crawl away into some weeds. The farmer assumed that was the end of the serpent. But a few days later the serpent reappeared, completely healed. The wise serpent had nibbled on the san qi weed, which stops internal and external bleeding.

和
冲

HARMONIES AND CONFLICTS

The twelve Taoist animal signs are grouped in four harmony triads to determine relationship compatibility. These triads indicate the most harmonious and desirable alliances between the animal signs. They are as follows:

```
          Rat                        Ox
          /\                         /\
         /  \                       /  \
  Dragon——Monkey          Serpent——Phoenix

         Tiger                      Hare
         /\                         /\
        /  \                       /  \
  Horse——Dog              Sheep——Boar
```

Note that there is a four- or eight-year age difference between each of the harmony triad signs. Interestingly, the harmony triads also correlate the Taoist signs with the Western astrological signs. There are striking resemblances in the way the signs of each system interact, although the two systems are unique and have many differences.

The Rat–Dragon–Monkey harmony triad correlates to the Western fire signs Sagittarius, Aries, and Leo, respectively. Rat, Dragon, and Monkey possess the extroverted personality traits associated with Western fire signs. They are dynamic, active, ag-

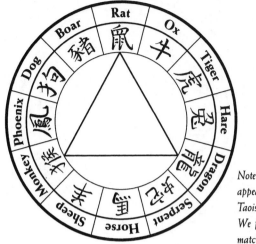

Note: traditionally Horse appears at the top of the Taoist astrological wheel. We placed Rat first to match the chronological progression of the signs.

gressive, passionate, vigorous, powerful, entertaining, and exhila-rating people. But at times they can be selfish, egocentric, and too dominating.

The Ox–Serpent–Phoenix harmony triad correlates to the West-ern earth signs Capricorn, Taurus, and Virgo, respectively. Ox, Ser-pent, and Phoenix possess the practical personality traits associated with Western earth signs. They are industrious, reliable, dedicated,

hardworking, mature, money-conscious, and success-oriented people. But at times they can be stubborn and narrow minded and may resist necessary change.

The Tiger–Horse–Dog harmony triad correlates to the Western air signs Aquarius, Gemini, and Libra, respectively. Tiger, Horse, and Dog possess the communicative personality traits associated with Western air signs. They are intelligent, rebellious, fair, fun-

loving, popular, social, funny, and lively. But at times they can be irresponsible and childish and can lack focus.

The Hare–Sheep–Boar harmony triad correlates to the Western water signs Pisces, Cancer, and Scorpio, respectively. Hare, Sheep, and Boar possess the sensitive personality traits associated with Western water signs. They are emotional, intuitive, empathetic, kind, compassionate, sentimental, nurturing, artistic, gentle, and loving people who feel deeply. But at times they can be indulgent, theatrical, and pessimistic.

An explanation of the astrological correlations is as follows:

Aries = Dragon. The fiery, dynamic Aries parallels the magnificent Dragon.

Taurus = Serpent. The sensuous, earthy Taurus parallels the wisdom and beauty of the Serpent.

Gemini = Horse. The carefree attitude of Gemini parallels the lively Horse personality.

Cancer = Sheep. The nurturing qualities of Cancer parallel the gentleness of the Sheep. (Some translations refer to Sheep as Ram or Goat, but Aries the Ram parallels Dragon and Capricorn the Goat parallels Ox.)

Leo = Monkey. The fire and drive of Leo parallel the winning ways of the Monkey.

Virgo = Phoenix. The analytical mind of Virgo parallels the thoroughness of the Phoenix.

Libra = Dog. The balance of Libran scales parallels the Dog's sense of justice and fair play.

Scorpio = Boar. The passionate nature of Scorpio parallels the Boar's devotion and lust for life.

Sagittarius = Rat. The adventuresome and philosophical Sagittarius parallels the curious and clever Rat.

Capricorn = Ox. The mature characteristics of Capricorn parallel the hardworking and diligent Ox.

Aquarius = Tiger. The unique, nonconformist Aquarius
parallels the spirited rebellious Tiger.

Pisces = Hare. The intuitive and kind Pisces parallels the
empathy and diplomacy of the Hare.

The three animal signs that share a harmony triad are most compatible because they possess equal values, ideals, and goals. Yet each animal sign is also compatible with one animal sign outside of their harmony trine. That compatible animal sign is as follows:

Rat: Rat favors Ox because Ox is reliable and dependable, offering Rat needed stability.

Ox: Ox favors Rat, even though Rat outwitted Ox in the old Taoist and Buddhist folktales (see page 47). Rat is good with money and keeps Ox entertained.

Tiger: Tiger favors Boar because Boar offers the sensuality, creativity, and affection that Tiger desires.

Hare: Hare favors Dog whose trust, loyalty, protection, and eagerness to help Hare develop her or his potential are valued by Hare.

Dragon: Dragon favors Phoenix because they make a harmonious pair whose vital energies are well matched. Dragon symbolizes the sky and Phoenix symbolizes the earth in a yang/yin balance.

Serpent: Serpent favors Monkey because Serpent's wisdom coupled with Monkey's guile make an unbeatable team.

Horse: Horse appreciates the gentility, charm, and beauty of Sheep who is willing to forgive Horse's selfishness.

Sheep: Sheep enjoys the companionship of Horse whose optimistic disposition helps Sheep be less pessimistic.

Monkey: Monkey favors Serpent because Serpent understands the Monkey mind and can use it to their mutual advantages.

Phoenix: Phoenix admires the power and majesty of Dragon.

Dragon and Phoenix together are a traditional
Chinese symbol of marriage.

Dog: Dog cherishes the peace and gentility offered by
Hare that helps Dog develop the yin Dog qualities.

Boar: Boar loves the wild Tiger who inspires Boar and
helps Boar when stuck with a problem or doubtful of
which way to proceed.

You are incompatible with the animal sign that is your opposite in the twelve-branch cycle. Note that there is a six-year age
difference with your incompatible opposite. In Western astrology, opposites can maintain a harmonious balance. But in Taoist
astrology, opposites are antagonistic opponents. Ironically, it is
from our opposite that we learn and succeed, by integrating their
qualities into our character. In this way, the balance of the Tao is
maintained.

Rat: Rat (Sagittarius) is opposite Horse (Gemini) in the
twelve-branch cycle. Horse's fun-loving, devil-may-
care attitude aggravates the thrifty, cautious Rat. Yet

Rat finds happiness by integrating Horse's innocence and optimism into Rat's character.

Ox: Ox (Capricorn) is opposite Sheep (Cancer) in the twelve-branch cycle. Dutiful Ox cannot comprehend Sheep's artistic, dreamy nature and love of artifice. Yet Ox progresses by valuing the Sheep characteristics of gentleness and purity.

Tiger: Tiger (Aquarius) is opposite Monkey (Leo) in the twelve-branch cycle. Antagonistic, sharp Monkey will tease (pull Tiger's tail) resulting in Tiger's anger. Yet Tiger learns by applying Monkey's cleverness and adaptability.

Hare: Hare (Pisces) is opposite Phoenix (Virgo) in the twelve-branch cycle. The blunt, often critical Phoenix communication feels like a bludgeoning beak on Hare's thin skin. Yet Hare develops strength by cultivating Phoenix qualities of toughness and directness.

Dragon: Dragon (Aries) is opposite Dog (Libra) in the twelve-branch cycle. Dragon's ego is not flattered by no-nonsense Dog, the only one not captivated by Dragon's magic and power. Yet Dragon evolves by learning the Dog qualities of ethical behavior and service to a higher cause.

Serpent: Serpent (Taurus) is opposite Boar (Scorpio) in the twelve-branch cycle. The calculating, psychological Serpent finds Boar to be one-dimensional and basic. Yet Serpent sheds her skin and transforms by integrating Boar qualities of honesty and simplicity.

Horse: Horse (Gemini) is opposite Rat (Sagittarius) in the twelve-branch cycle. Horse's need for freedom, change, and variety is not understood by materialistic Rat. Yet Horse matures by cultivating Rat qualities of thrift and acquisitiveness.

Sheep: Sheep (Cancer) is opposite Ox (Capricorn) in the

twelve-branch cycle. Sheep's artistic sensibilities find Ox slow witted, boring, and too conservative. Yet Sheep succeeds by developing Ox qualities of discipline and hard work.

Monkey: Monkey (Leo) is opposite Tiger (Aquarius) in the twelve-branch cycle. Monkey views Tiger as a spoilsport and poor loser. Yet Monkey heals by copying Tiger's bravery and altruism.

Phoenix: Phoenix (Virgo) is opposite Hare (Pisces) in the twelve-branch cycle. Phoenix perceives Hare as being too weak and soft for diligent, determined Phoenix. Yet Phoenix is reborn through cultivating Hare's diplomatic and demure nature.

Dog: Dog (Libra) is opposite Dragon (Aries) in the twelve-branch cycle. To realistic Dog, Dragon's style appears to be glory and flash without substance. Yet Dog betters her- or himself by developing the Dragon qualities of self-interest and by enjoying healthy dreams and fantasies.

Boar: Boar (Scorpio) is opposite Serpent (Taurus) in the twelve-branch cycle. Good-natured Boar does not relate well to the intense and complex Serpent. Yet Boar grows by learning the Serpent qualities of reflection and introspection.

In determining relationship compatibility, also examine the Taoist element (see page 26) and the rising-sign animal (see page 14). These relationship guidelines may be very helpful in problem solving and healing of disruptive energies that can be transformed through conscious action and pure intention. But when living in accordance with the Tao, all things are compatible and create a harmonious balance according to their cycles and seasons.

TWO

The Twelve Earthly Branches

RAT

*Key words: Quick mind, a good
bargainer, a natural
charmer.
Rat correlates to the Western sign
Sagittarius.*

RAT LUNAR CALENDAR

1900—January 31 to February 18, 1901   White Rat
1912—February 18 to February 5, 1913   Black Rat
1924—February 5 to January 24, 1925   Green Rat
1936—January 24 to February 10, 1937   Red Rat
1948—February 10 to January 28, 1949   Yellow Rat
1960—January 28 to February 14, 1961   White Rat
1972—February 15 to February 1, 1973   Black Rat
1984—February 2 to February 18, 1985   Green Rat
1996—February 19 to February 5, 1997   Red Rat
2008—February 2 to January 25, 2009   Yellow Rat
2020—January 25 to February 11, 2021   White Rat

RAT YEAR

Clever, magnificent Rat is honored in Asian culture, unlike the
Western stereotype of rats as plague-carrying vermin to be exter-
minated. In Japanese lore, a white (metal) Rat is the symbol of
Daikoku, the god of wealth and prosperity. Therefore, Rat has the

natural ability to be successful. Although some translations refer to Rat as mouse, this is misleading because Rat's personality is rarely meek and mousy.

The most significant Rat character trait is cleverness. A Taoist folktale recalls how Rat conquered Ox and became the first animal of the Taoist zodiac.

There was a contest in a Chinese village to select the twelve animals of the horoscope. Ox was working on a farm when Rat came to see him. Rat told Ox about the contest because he wanted to ride on Ox's back to get to the village.

Ox trudged for miles over difficult terrain with Rat on his back. Ox struggled as he swam across a mighty river with Rat on his back. When Ox and Rat finally arrived at the village, people saw Rat riding on the back of Ox. They were so impressed by this that they made Rat number one in the sequence of the twelve animals.

In a Buddhist version of this Taoist folktale, the first animal to the bedside of the dying Buddha would be made the first animal of the zodiac. Rat rode on Ox's back then, as Ox approached the bedside, Rat jumped off and got there first. Rat has been the first animal ever since.

The year of the Rat is a time of plenty, bringing abundance and good fortune. In this auspicious year, some of Rat's prosperity can influence everyone, regardless of one's birth animal. Expect a powerful year, when people are firm about their goals, passions, and aspirations. Although there may be fluctuation in world economies, it is an excellent time to start a business, buy property, invest in long-term plans, or accumulate wealth. All ventures begun in Rat years will prosper if well prepared. But it is not a time for foolish risks—save those for Tiger and Monkey years. Rat loves the pack, so it is also a time for socializing, entertaining, and enjoying ourselves.

RAT PERSONALITY

The person born in a Rat year is clever, sharp, humorous, creative, industrious, curious, intuitive, witty, optimistic, yet frugal. He can pinch pennies and is a great bargainer. The Rat individual is very observant, quick to take action, and popular in social circles. Rat's charm and quick wit often wins admiration wherever he goes. Rat can adapt easily to different environments and can survive against all odds.

Rat is very instinctive and relies on instinct and cleverness to succeed. But Rat must not ignore logic and reality and become caught in an unrealistic rat trap. Because Rat is so intelligent, his racing mind can create an illogical maze. Sometimes Rat's active mind becomes like a rodent on a treadmill, endlessly running but going nowhere. At these times, Rat must avoid the negative traits of being sly, secretive, critical, and judgmental of others. Rat can create internal stress when he worries and frets endlessly, especially about health.

Since Rat is a nocturnal animal, he often enjoys working at night during the quiet hours. But staying up all night can cause health problems. Yet Rat loves to stay up until the wee hours, for that is Rat's creative time. Rat has a natural talent for the arts, specifically writing.

Rat has a great appetite and appreciates fine cuisine. He loves all types of tasty food, fine wines, baked goods, and luxurious gourmet meals. Although Rat may not have the patience to prepare these fine meals, he will be first in line at the newest restaurant.

RAT RELATIONSHIPS

Rat with Rat: Two entertaining Rats can create an intimate Rat pack. Each can share much affection and tenderness with the other. Both are sharp, quick, and clever and enjoy a great togetherness. But two Rats must avoid criticizing each other during difficult moments. Rat learns more with a partner of a different sign.

Rat with Ox: Rat finds a strong ally in the solid Ox. Even though

Rat outwitted Ox in the old folktale they are still close friends. Security-conscious Ox understands Rat's need to hoard. They admire each other's tough qualities; Rat likes the dependability and good-provider role of Ox, while Ox relishes the clever problem-solving capabilities of Rat. Ox enjoys being fussed over by Rat and loves affectionate Rat's attention. This relationship can last a lifetime.

Rat with Tiger: Rat may not enjoy the companionship of Tiger because Rat does not trust Tiger and resents Tiger's spontaneity and impulsiveness. Rat is too cautious and calculating to behave rashly. Extravagant Tiger may consider thrifty Rat too cheap. If Rat complains or accuses Tiger of selfishness, Tiger could retaliate and abuse Rat. A light social bond may be enjoyable, but a deeper relationship may prove problematic.

Rat with Hare: Rat and peaceful Hare can be amiable. But they have very different values, especially concerning the spending of money. Rat saves, Hare spends. If they can compromise on a financial arrangement, Rat will feel secure. Their temperaments differ; Rat is an indulgent adventurer and Hare is an artistic homebody. But if their love is deep enough, they can create a storybook romance with much affection and mutual caring.

Rat with Dragon: Rat is useful to the mighty Dragon and together they can achieve success and prosperity. Their future together will improve in time. Both are loyal and trust each other. Since trust is not an easy emotion for Rat, trust will be one of the many glues that binds their relationship. Dragon admires Rat's thrift and resourcefulness as well as Rat's talkative, flowing charm. Sexually, this is a most passionate and exciting combination for Rat.

Rat with Serpent: Rat admires Serpent's strength and power. Serpent's insight and wisdom can help Rat avoid traps and mazes. In return, Serpent admires Rat's cleverness and ambition to succeed. Serpent appreciates a partner who can provide charm, devotion, and romance. Sexually, they are often extremely compatible. Both will cooperate because mutually they have much to gain from each other. But they must avoid controlling behavior, especially if Serpent wraps too tightly around Rat.

Rat with Horse: Horse may be the worst possible mate for Rat. Horse's fun-loving, devil-may-care attitude aggravates the cautious Rat. They disagree on most issues, and neither is willing to concede defeat. Rat's worst traits surface and he becomes conniving, competitive, and dishonest. Similarly in Rat's company, Horse behaves with selfishness, stubbornness, and resentment. In this union, neither can be happy and both will feel misunderstood. Avoid Horse, who is Rat's opposite.

Rat with Sheep: Rat and Sheep are immediately attracted to each other because they are both so charming. In a crowded room, Rat will find lovely Sheep and Sheep will find engaging Rat. But problems can surface quickly. Rat is a hard worker, and Sheep dislikes any type of labor. Sheep "eat paper," meaning that Sheep spends money on luxuries. Thrifty Rat will not tolerate Sheep's indulgences. Sensitive Sheep can be wounded easily by Rat's criticism and calculating ways. A serious commitment between Rat and Sheep may prove very challenging.

Rat with Monkey: Rat and Monkey are an excellent combination for happiness. Rat is fascinated by the entertaining and ingenious Monkey. In return, Monkey admires Rat for being a go-getter and achiever. Wily Monkey's trickiness is forgiven by the usually suspicious Rat because Rat understands Monkey's motives. They are on the same wavelength. Because they can communicate directly, problems can be circumvented before they fester. But Rat must keep Monkey stimulated, for Monkey will not stay if bored.

Rat with Phoenix: These two distinct personalities cannot communicate. They are a fight waiting to happen. Each criticizes the other in an endless power struggle. Phoenix likes to win, and Rat may be shocked when Phoenix attempts to manipulate Rat into submission. They are both too intelligent and bossy to concede to the other. Perhaps they can combine their brains in a work situation, but a romance may be very difficult.

Rat with Dog: These two instinctive types possess the similar values of independence and hard work. Both are intelligent and affectionate. Practical Rat teaches Dog to be less idealistic and to enjoy life. Loyal Dog is a positive influence who teaches Rat to have higher scruples. They can make a good team while respecting each other's privacy.

Rat with Boar: Rat has much to gain in this union. Rat can rely on the sturdy Boar. Both share common goals and can create a close and intimate relationship. Both are social, fun loving, and great gourmands. Together they can host many parties since both cultivate myriad friendships. But Rat should be a little less aggressive with the kind-hearted Boar, who is a gentle soul.

RAT CHILD AND PARENT

The Rat child will be intelligent, a fast learner, and an early talker. He will love creative ideas that stimulate young Rat's sharp mind and imagination, so reading to your Rat child is highly recommended. A Rat born in the spring, summer, or fall has an easier time in life, for that is when grain is plentiful and food is easy to find. But a Rat born in the cold of winter also can have abundance, for that is when the harvest bins are full of grain. A Rat born at night is very active and has a more hectic life than a daytime-born Rat. A daytime-born Rat may have an easier life and find peace.

The Rat parent dotes on her or his child and is very attentive to her or his offspring's every need. Rat is intelligent and cultivates that quality in children. Therefore, Rat parents will read to their children and invest in their education. The same rules of compatibility apply as for Rat relationships: Rat favors Dragon, Monkey, and Ox children, who will excel in school and be successful. Rat is compatible with Rat, Hare, Serpent, Dog, and Boar children, who will obey Rat's rules and acquiesce to Rat's standards. But Horse, Tiger, Sheep, and Phoenix children could create strain and problems for the Rat parent. Care must be taken by the Rat parent not to display favoritism. Instead, strive to honor all children equally.

RAT IN THE TWELVE-BRANCH CYCLE

Rat in Rat year: This time brings good fortune, abundance, and luck. Financial gain is foreseen, happiness and contentment can be found, and creativity is stimulated. Rat is empowered by experiencing his own year.

Rat in Ox year: Expect a pleasant year with few hardships or troubles because Ox is Rat's good friend. But a larger contribution may be expected at work because the Ox influence indicates hard labor.

Rat in Tiger year: Expect to do well, but the impulsive energy of a Tiger year could be a confusing or unstable influence for the usually cautious Rat. A year to be pragmatic and avoid confrontation. Lawsuits are not favored at this time.

Rat in Hare year: Expect peace and tranquillity in a Hare year. Rat will succeed in business endeavors and enlarge his circle of friends, family, and influence.

Rat in Dragon year: Expect achievement, success, and good fortune in all endeavors, especially relationships and career. Dragon is Rat's best friend, so powerful Dragon energy will assist Rat. This may be one of Rat's best years of the twelve-branch cycle and is an excellent time for marriage.

Rat in Serpent year: Expect a sobering year when Rat must limit the grandiosity of the previous Dragon year and adjust to living more simply. Take care to not overspend or over extend. Practicality will be rewarded and bring success.

Rat in Horse year: Prepare for the most uncomfortable year of the entire twelve-branch cycle because Horse is Rat's one enemy. Be very cautious in all dealings, especially legal and financial. This is not an auspicious year for marriage.

Rat in Sheep year: Expect to recover from previous Horse-year difficulties. New opportunities arise and clever Rat can recognize and capitalize on the money floating around in a Sheep year. Life will become more comfortable, and Rat may find peace.

Rat in Monkey year: Expect a fun, exciting year full of Monkey-inspired surprises. Monkey is Rat's close friend and this may be one of the best years of the twelve-branch cycle. Labors from past years bear fruit. This is an excellent year for marriage.

Rat in Phoenix year: Expect a festive and fun year; a continuation of the good fortune from the previous Monkey year. But Phoenix's influence, like Ox's influence, requires Rat to work harder and contribute more at work.

Rat in Dog year: Expect a somewhat difficult year, but not as trying as a Horse year. Rat's individuality is curtailed and he must comply with the wishes of the majority. Avoid a pessimistic or critical attitude, especially concerning relationships.

Rat in Boar year: Expect a year for planning instead of achieving. Boar year is a time for Rat to rest, indulge, and recoup from past losses. It is best to reserve energy for next year when the twelve-branch cycle begins anew in the Rat year.

火 RED RAT—1936, 1996

鼠 Red Rat is the fire Rat. When fire expresses masculine yang energy, it is symbolized by burning wood. If you were born in the year of the red Rat, burning wood is your creative symbol.

Fire qualities are reason, expressiveness, spirituality, intuition, insight, dynamism, passion, aggressiveness, leadership, and a proper sense of etiquette (see page 18). Since these are natural Rat characteristics, red Rat has little problem with self-expression. Red Rat's original personality is appreciated by many who view him as a passionate and daring individual.

Red Rat possesses endless enthusiasm and energy for activities and affairs. He has the potential to be very serious and singularly focused. Of all Rats, red Rat is the one most apt to convert ideas into action. Forceful ways often lead to commercial prosperity. Red Rat can get the best deal and figure out the quickest way out of the maze to find success.

Red Rat lives a life of extremes. If red Rat's fire burns too brightly, he may passionately begin projects that later prove too monumental to complete. Excessive fieriness can also manifest as lack of discipline and refusal of any restraints. An excellent way for red Rat to use that boundless energy and lust for life is by traveling and seeing the world.

Red Rat makes judgments based on witnessed actions. He avoids emotional issues because feelings are confusing. Feelings and sympathy are in the realm of the element water, which is Rat's earthly branch (see page 22). Water extinguishes fire; therefore red Rat usually experiences much inner emotional turmoil. To heal this dilemma, experiences that are fun, joyful, loving, and pleasurable should be pursued by red Rat.

Red Rat is very direct, at times blunt, and can be very verbal with opinions and ideas. If one quarrels with red Rat, one finds a very conniving and ruthless foe. After much bluster and dramatics, red Rat may not follow through with threats because he has lost interest. Red Rat must balance the tendency to exaggerate, lie, or charm to win favor. Red Rat benefits by sharing his warmhearted generosity and being less severe with weaker people.

YELLOW RAT—1948, 2008

 Yellow Rat is the earth Rat. When earth expresses masculine yang energy, it is symbolized by a hill. If you were born in the year of the yellow Rat, a hill or mountain is your personal symbol.

Earth qualities include stability, honesty, practicality, industry, prudence, reliability, kindness, and loyalty (see page 20). These qualities enrich yellow Rat's character, making him more trustworthy, reliable, and sincere than other Rats. Earth makes yellow Rat "down to earth," and not too flamboyant or overly enthusiastic about extreme schemes and plans. Yellow Rat is willing to work harder than other Rats—who would rather connive their way to success—in order to be recognized for accomplishments. Yellow Rat rarely manipulates others to attain a goal. Instead, he respects the bonds of friendship, is sincere and faithful, and can sacrifice for the common good.

The sign of the Rat is action oriented. But Rat's earthly branch is the element water (see page 22). Earth blocks water, so the yellow Rat is slowed down, more methodical, thorough, calm, and pragmatic than other Rats. Yellow Rat dislikes change and wild adventures. He achieves success in small, well-deserved increments. He does well in service-oriented work that satisfies both the emotional and dramatic side of the Rat personality and the industrious nature found in those born during the earth year. Yellow Rat succeeds by staying in one career or one place long enough to establish roots and build security. Yellow Rat is security conscious, desires success, and will endlessly compare his achievements to those of colleagues. Cautious yellow Rat is not a money lender, gambler, big spender, or financially generous. Like all Rats, yellow Rat will hoard.

The earth element is stabilizing for yellow Rat, making a calmer and less erratic Rat. Yellow Rat does well to meditate and contemplate. It is important for yellow Rat to nurture himself physically, emotionally, and spiritually. But yellow Rat can become overly focused and intolerant of other's methodologies, especially if yellow Rat is working under a deadline. Yellow Rat must curb the Rat tendency toward selfishness and self-promoting schemes. Instead, yellow Rat succeeds by demonstrating a sympathetic nature and showing great kindness to others.

WHITE RAT—1900, 1960

White Rat is the metal Rat. Metal, when it expresses masculine yang energy, is symbolized by a weapon. If you were born in the year of the white Rat, a weapon is your personal symbol.

Metal qualities are righteousness, independence, strong will, intensity, uprightness, determination, and ability to focus (see page 21). These powerful qualities add to white Rat's ability to survive. But these same qualities can create a dynamic person who does not reveal ulterior motives. White Rat's kind personality often masks a jealous, possessive, and competitive soul obsessed with achieving success, getting the best deal, and desiring to win at any cost.

White Rat exhibits all of the best and worst qualities of a Rat individual, being the most developed, yet obvious, Rat. Water is Rat's earthly branch (see page 22). The element metal nurtures and contains water, which is advantageous for white Rat. White Rat can succeed easily and achieve set goals.

White Rat is excellent in business and investments, yet can be jealous of others' successes. He is a talker who possesses a very entertaining and engaging personality. All Rats are charmers, so white Rat can eloquently flatter, praise, and cajole.

When challenged, white Rat can become brassy, excessively talkative or loud, aggressive, and argumentative. Such extreme behavior is not to white Rat's advantage in business. White Rat may appear slightly cold due to the influence of metal, at times being callous or a bit gruff.

White Rat often creates unbalanced relationships of codependence in order to wield power over partners. White Rat does well to allow partners some independence and not be stubborn, selfish, and always wanting his own way. Romance and frivolity will not be in his nature if such antics cost money and don't leave tangible results.

White Rat's passion and fervor border on religiosity. He feels all experiences very deeply and is willing to discuss felt emotions.

White Rat dislikes hard work, especially menial labor, and desires housekeepers, nannies, and gardeners. This will impress others while keeping white Rat free to decorate, dress well, and connive ways to lure influential people. White Rat is a very warm and emotional person, but only to those who can help him succeed.

White Rat is a sensualist and connoisseur of all life has to offer. Therefore, he will spend money, which is not a typical Rat trait. White Rat desires only the finest of all material goods, yet seeks to acquire them at bargain rates and does not like to share. He will hoard, be obsessive about money and social achievement, and desire get-rich-quick investment schemes.

White Rat succeeds by being less opinionated, accepting change, and gracefully releasing the past. The white Rat challenge is to express emotions, including grief, and find his own way of healing.

水 鼠 BLACK RAT—1912, 1972

Black Rat is the water Rat. Water, when it expresses masculine yang energy, is symbolized by a wave. If you were born in the year of the black Rat, your personal symbol is a cresting wave.

Water qualities are sensitivity, drive, effectiveness, creativity, passion for life and sex, valuing family and social contacts, and the potential to attract. With a double dose of water qualities, black Rat is heavily influenced by the element water, Rat's earthly branch (see page 22). Thus, black Rat is more flexible, adaptable, and amiable, acquiescing to the wishes of others, unlike other Rats. Yet Rats of other colors might consider black Rat the weakest Rat because he is not ruthless and does not value money over friendship, emotions, and love.

Black Rat is extremely emotional and not always rational. He is an intuitive, in touch with his feelings and desires. Ruled by this nature, indecisive black Rat can be self-doubting. The least successful in business and the most volatile in relationships, black Rat is a survivor and can overcome any obstacle if he is true to his emotions.

Black Rat's well-developed water qualities lead to much expression of emotion and an empathetic understanding of relationship intricacies. When properly channeled, these qualities can lead to the creation of a great artist or writer. A black Rat without a creative vehicle can become excessive when expressing emotions or will express them in inappropriate social settings. This type of overly emotional black Rat benefits from the healing arts and learns much from the psychological therapeutic process.

Black Rat is a natural scholar, student, and intellectual who loves to learn and could succeed in an academic career. When too mentally stimulated, black Rat can be frantic or overactive, especially if black Rat was born at night. All Rats are naturally talented writers, but black Rat is especially suited to succeed as a writer due to sharp skills of observation and an empathetic nature. Black Rat is happy when writing, speaking, and relating to people from all walks of life. Black Rat can also be a sensitive and caring healer. Being shrewd, like all Rats, black Rat will succeed in any chosen profession and will curry favor to succeed. Although water softens the typical Rat traits of ruthlessness and selfishness, black Rat will use his sensitivity to his advantage. He can be the most flexible, charming, and sensuous of all Rats.

Water can make black Rat passive, shy, and timid. He prefers to stay home in his secure nest to write, read, and study in peace, but black Rat must venture into the world and interact with many others to succeed. Black Rat's challenge is to overcome this fear and become an active participant in life. Black Rat may be the happiest of Rats, able to overcome many obstacles and still satisfy both the sensual and philosophical sides.

GREEN RAT—1924, 1984

Green Rat is the wood Rat. When wood expresses masculine yang energy, it is symbolized by a pine tree, sturdy and upright. If you were born in the year of the green Rat, the pine is your totem.

Wood qualities include boldness, creativity, idealism, imagination, planning, decision making, steadfastness, benevolence, and competitiveness (see page 24). Wood types initiate new projects and possess the ability to complete them, seldom wavering from a chosen path. These are natural Rat characteristics, so a green Rat easily achieves established goals.

Rat's earthly branch is water (see page 22). This alchemy is to green Rat's advantage because water feeds wood. This makes green Rat creative, progressive, idealistic, and able to succeed. Green Rat's winning personality, self-confidence, and quickness of wit enable him to achieve professional acclaim and much reward.

Green Rat is very impatient and wants everything immediately. A disciplined Rat who overachieves, green Rat is driven by fear of scarcity and fantasizes about a huge hoard of money and property. He does well to temper selfish tendencies and myopic vision while pursuing a goal.

Green Rat understands how businesses and hierarchies work. He can quickly assess the quickest way out of the maze to grab the prized cheese. Green Rat can be adaptable, if for no other reason than to stay in favor with those whose opinions matter. Unfortunately, in business or personal affairs, green Rat may move too quickly for others to keep up. Green Rat can be stubborn, prejudiced, and relentless. He will not suffer fools gladly and may need to practice understanding of others and their human foibles.

Adventurous and brave, green Rat fears little. This individual is an inspired and inquisitive traveler who makes the best of even the most taxing situations. Like all Rats, green Rat is a good talker. But unlike most Rats, green Rat can talk his way to success without having to perform any duties or possess the required skills. Green Rat may employ deceit if ambition is not checked.

Green Rat is happiest when flexible and open-minded. Green Rat's challenge is to control and channel anger into positive actions for the benefit of others.

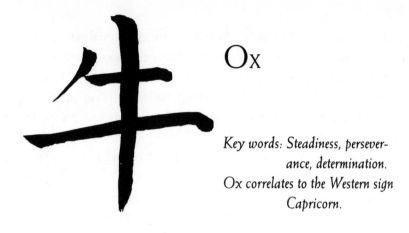

Ox

*Key words: Steadiness, persever-
ance, determination.
Ox correlates to the Western sign
Capricorn.*

Ox Lunar Calendar

1901—February 19 to February 7, 1902 Silver Ox
1913—February 6 to January 25, 1914   Gray Ox
1925—January 25 to February 12, 1926 Blue Ox
1937—February 11 to January 30, 1938 Purple Ox
1949—January 29 to February 16, 1950 Gold Ox
1961—February 15 to February 4, 1962 Silver Ox
1973—February 3 to January 22, 1974   Gray Ox
1985—February 20 to February 8, 1986 Blue Ox
1997—February 7 to January 27, 1998   Purple Ox
2009—January 26 to February 13, 2010 Gold Ox
2021—February 12 to January 31, 2022 Silver Ox

Ox Year

Ox and all cattle are blessed by the compassionate Chinese goddess Kwan Yin because of their gentle, peaceful nature (Kwan Yin
is known as Kwannon in Japan). The ancient Taoists harnessed the
Ox, but didn't milk it, for they honored this strong, hardworking
animal. The mythical golden-haired Ox king, Niu Wang, protected
cattle from epidemics. In the Buddhist tradition the white Ox sym-

bolizes contemplation and wisdom. Some translations refer to Ox as buffalo, water buffalo, bull (male), or cow (female).

According to an ancient Taoist legend, humans have a special relationship with Ox. In early agricultural communities, people often went for days without eating and feared starvation. To aid suffering humans, the Gods and Goddesses removed Ox from heaven, where she was a star, and sent her to earth. The divine ones instructed Ox to tell people that with her help they would avoid starvation and would eat every three days. Ox misunderstood and told humanity that they would eat three times a day. Ox had to make her words true, and that is why Ox must labor so hard for people and endure many burdens without complaint.

The year of the Ox is time for hard work. Like Ox plowing the fields, we must toil during this year. Success is attained through diligent work and conscientious effort. Begin by putting your affairs in order, especially your home. Stick to routine, tried-and-true methods, and conservative actions. Wild, new concepts will not be well received (save them for the following Tiger year). Ox year is not a time for laziness. Those who won't work, won't eat. But if we refrain from rebelling, follow the rules, and try to obey authorities, there will be a bountiful harvest. Expect conservative politics.

Ox Personality

The person born in an Ox year is methodical, dependable, hardworking, patient, diligent, and ethical. She is independent, steadfast, and careful. She won't take action before having carefully thought through the entire project and planned out every detail. Ox believes in achieving goals step by step. Once Ox sets a goal, she won't relent until the objective is attained. Possessing high morals and standards, Ox has integrity and can be trusted. Ox is usually self-reliant, believes deeply in what she does, and has faith in her ability to get the job done. She is noted for determination in accomplishing tasks. The Ox individual doesn't seek shortcuts and sometimes disrespects those who do. Ox is generally an honest person with strong values.

Like underground seeds struggling to grow toward the

sunlight, Ox can find life's journey laborious and the rewards uncertain. Ox believes that if she applies herself and performs, she will be recognized and rewarded. Ox firmly perseveres and is not swayed easily by other people's opinions. Rarely does Ox make an effort to seek social connections to achieve success. But in today's work environment, where advancement often depends on how you sell yourself, Ox may have to wait a long time to get her just rewards. In this circumstance, the Ox individual can feel underappreciated. But Ox must not become bitter and frustrated because of this, for the Ox temperament can do even more damage to hinder success.

Ox can make a dependable and loyal friend or mate. If you have a friend born in an Ox year, don't be defensive when she bluntly points out your flaws. Ox is not afraid to speak candidly and won't soften criticism to spare your feelings. It is her way of expressing that she cares.

In relationship, Ox is a good provider. It is better for Ox to be pursued than to be the hunter in selecting a mate. The surprises and thrills of romance may not be Ox's forte because she may not be overtly romantic. Nor is Ox the first to try new things, set trends, or take the initiative. Ox is home oriented and appreciates both a secure home and work environment. Ox enjoys feasts and snacks, and often overeats out of habit. To Ox, it's not overeating, just grazing.

Stubbornness is the most negative Ox trait. Ox will go to great lengths to prove that she is right, sometimes at the risk of breaking a friendship or hurting other people's feelings. Even though Ox appears peaceful and at ease most of the time, anger Ox at your own risk and face the wrath of a wild bull.

Ox Relationships

Ox with Rat: Ox finds a strong ally in the sharp Rat, even though Rat outwitted Ox in the old Taoist folktale (see page 47). Ox respects Rat's thrifty ways and intelligent counsel. The social and romantic Rat brings Ox out of her conservative shell. Rat

is a good provider, which Ox deems necessary for a serious relationship. This partnership can last a lifetime.

Ox with Ox: Two Oxen have similar interests and values. They enjoy a peaceful home, are materialistic and conservative, and enjoy mutual trust and respect. Their life together may become a bit boring and staid, but they will create stability and security. If stubborn Oxen fight, a struggle for dominance could result.

Ox with Tiger: Ox may find Tiger too impulsive and daring, and not to be trusted. These two lack understanding of each other's motives and may not share common goals. Ox may become serious and somber while trying to discipline Tiger, who resents being controlled. Tiger may be too passionate for reticent Ox, and Tiger requires more passion than Ox can give. Both are big, powerful, stubborn, strong-willed, and defensive— a clash is to be expected. Ox insists on winning and will in this combination.

Ox with Hare: Ox and kindly Hare could make a solid team. Hare relies on dependable Ox for protection and will follow Ox's orders. Ox's firmness is viewed with a sense of humor by the amiable Hare. Both enjoy a lovely home, and Hare teaches Ox how to appreciate the arts. Ox enjoys Hare's affection and gentleness. Together they can create a warm and caring relationship.

But Ox should pamper sensitive Hare, understand Hare's need to indulge, and avoid direct criticism.

Ox with Dragon: Gentle Ox wants peace and tranquillity, which cannot be had with a Dragon partner. Extroverted Dragon enjoys a life full of dazzle and surprise; the unexpected may be traumatic for stable Ox. Dragon wishes to be admired; Ox is too practical for such silliness. Ox is slow; Dragon is fast. Between these two very strong animals, both want to be the boss. They are basically incompatible, yet respect each other in business.

Ox with Serpent: Ox keeps the home fires burning while Serpent is out in the world of action and intrigue. Each values the sympathy, caring, and understanding that the other provides. Together they can create intimacy through conversation. Wise Serpent likes to ponder and discuss while Ox enjoys listening and learning. Both Ox and Serpent are down-to-earth types who rely on each other. Serpent lives up to Ox's high moral standards, which is not an easy feat.

Ox with Horse: Horse may not share Ox's family and home-oriented concerns. Ox values security and constancy, which are not Horse's strong points. Horse requires freedom, while Ox desires stability. Ox enjoys building a steady partnership, but impatient Horse doesn't have the time. Adventurous Horse may find Ox slow and unwilling to take risks. If a power struggle results, independent Horse will resist being dominated. They cannot have fun together, and Horse loves fun.

Ox with Sheep: The worst combination for Ox is with artistic Sheep. Little Sheep's capricious, fun-loving nature and dislike of hard work bothers dependable Ox. Solid Ox prefers a routine schedule and plans events carefully. Sheep considers every day a new adventure and would find a normal routine unbearable. Ox works hard at acquiring money; Sheep "eats paper," meaning that Sheep spends more than she earns. If Ox tries to guide or discipline unmanageable Sheep, she will leave abruptly. Avoid Sheep, who is Ox's opposite.

Ox with Monkey: Ox can learn about life from Monkey. Ox is mesmerized by Monkey's quick wit, entertaining personality, and passionate sexuality. Clever Monkey knows every short-cut and can show Ox easier ways to succeed. In return, Monkey can benefit from Ox's stabilizing influence. But Ox must be patient with Monkey. Time will indicate whether or not honest Ox can trust Monkey.

Ox with Phoenix: Ox creates a secure home environment while Phoenix is out in the working world achieving success. Ox becomes inspired to work harder, which pleases Phoenix. During difficult times, often scattered Phoenix can rely on sturdy Ox. Ox and Phoenix can express themselves in a frank and direct manner without hurting each other. In this relationship, Ox will be appreciated for all her hard work and sacrifice.

Ox with Dog: Ox and Dog share similar qualities of loyalty and faithfulness. They can trust and rely on each other. Ox can learn much from the supportive and open-minded Dog. But compromise may be necessary. Both are independent, but Dog requires more independence than Ox. Ox should realize that independence does not mean lack of love. Ox wants to run the home, and Dog does best to accept Ox's rule and declare a truce.

Ox with Boar: Ox and pleasant Boar can be cordial to each other. Both are loyal and value a secure home. Ox admires Boar's direct honesty and sincerity. Boar appreciates Ox's dependability and fortitude. Boar can teach Ox how to relax and be more affectionate. And Boar allows Ox to organize Boar's chaos. But theirs may not be a lasting bond; Boar cannot indulge her fine tastes with conservative Ox.

Ox Child and Parent

The Ox child will be a tough kid, not a crybaby, who can endure hardship without complaint. She enjoys privacy, is expected to be a late talker, and enjoys physical, outdoor activities. Ox child appreciates discipline and a routine schedule administered by dependable parents. Impulsive surprises and sudden changes in plans are seen as threats to security. Ox children born in the winter, after the crops are harvested, have an easier life. But the spring- and summer-born Ox labors and plows the fields, meaning she must work hard to accomplish tasks. Life may be easier for the night-born Ox who can rest from daytime labors.

The Ox parent will organize a child's life and schedule all activities. Balanced meals can be expected at the same time every day. The no-nonsense Ox parent expects children to follow rules and routines. Ox's children will be rewarded if they conform, earn good grades, dress conservatively, etc. The same rules of compatibility apply as for Ox relationships: Ox favors Serpent, Phoenix, and Rat children, who perform best due to the stability of strong family security. Ox, Hare, Dog, and Boar children will comply and obey, but Tiger, Dragon, Monkey, Horse, and Sheep children would rather rebel. If an Ox parent doesn't ease up on the rules with these artistic types, rebellion could cause family problems. Ox instinct may be to clamp down harder. Then there may be the risk of a runaway child, especially a Horse child.

OX IN THE TWELVE-BRANCH CYCLE

Ox in Rat year: Expect good fortune and prosperity. Financial gain, recognition, and promotion are foreseen. Rat is Ox's good friend; therefore, friends and associates will be helpful and beneficial.

Ox in Ox year: Expect a positive and productive year. Ox's hard work will be rewarded because Ox is empowered by experiencing her own year. Excellent for starting a family.

Ox in Tiger year: Expect the unexpected. This is not the easiest time for Ox. Although others may take wild risks and enjoy caprices, it is not in Ox's best interests to do so.

Ox in Hare year: This is the time to recover from last year's difficulties. Peace shall be found, health can improve, and affairs will flow more smoothly with fewer personal conflicts.

Ox in Dragon year: Fireworks may go off around you but avoid the festivities. Ox must work hard and be very focused, dedicated, patient, and reliable. Rewards come at the end of the year.

Ox in Serpent year: Expect a great year because Serpent is Ox's dear friend. A time for opportunity, expansion, good luck, and growth. But Ox must avoid being the subject of gossip, scandal, or secrets.

Ox in Horse year: Chaos and confusion surround you. Money may be tight, difficulties unforeseen, and Ox could become overextended trying to help others. Avoid excessive work, especially in summer when Ox toils in the fields.

Ox in Sheep year: Expect delays and setbacks. Events may progress slowly. Ox is hardworking and Sheep is not. Under Sheep's influence, perhaps not much can be accomplished. Try to remain even tempered.

Ox in Monkey year: Wily Monkey influence brings calamity and misadventure. Ox's methods may not be appreciated, but if Ox stays true to her values and convictions when faced with adversity, she will be rewarded.

Ox in Phoenix year: Expect good times because Phoenix is Ox's friend and ally. Work is challenging but rewarding, family life is harmonious, and Ox can be recognized for her contributions.

Ox in Dog year: Expect problems with others that can be resolved through honest communication and attention to duty. It may seem that as soon as one issue is resolved, another problem appears, but no problem is so overwhelming that Ox cannot handle it properly.

Ox in Boar year: Expect much activity, both at home and in business. Ox is motivated and stimulated by the extra work. New contacts and opportunities appear that may be very beneficial.

火牛 Purple Ox—1937, 1997

Purple Ox is the fire Ox. When fire expresses feminine yin energy, it is symbolized by the flame of a lamp. If you were born in the year of the purple Ox, a pure flame is your personal symbol of purity for meditation.

Fire qualities are reason, expressiveness, spirituality, intuition, insight, dynamism, passion, aggressiveness, leadership, and a proper sense of etiquette (see page 18). These characteristics add great range of expression to purple Ox. She is honest, powerful, and dedicated to work and loved ones. Purple Ox is not a parasite and strives to make an effective long-lasting contribution to society.

Her unrestrained passion, aggressiveness, and desire to lead guarantees success in all endeavors, but purple Ox often overwhelms others who work in a more cooperative manner. If purple Ox cannot be in control, she can exhibit a very bad, fiery temper. It is at these times when purple Ox benefits by remembering her pure flame symbol, releasing her desire for material goods, and replacing desire with compassion.

The release of desire can be a difficult challenge for purple Ox, who desperately wishes to achieve power, importance, status—even fame. While pursuing goals, purple Ox can become proud, selfish, and demanding. Desiring to win any competition, purple Ox can be arrogant, self-satisfied, and vain. When obsessed with material success, purple Ox will value money more than spiritual insight. All Oxen are materialistic, but the purple Ox can be excessively so.

Water is Ox's earthly branch (see page 22). Water extinguishes fire, which is not advantageous for purple Ox. This alchemy results in her emotional expression being thwarted. Therefore, purple Ox can possess little regard for the emotions or contributions of others. She can be very dismissive of those who cannot immediately help her to attain status in society. Water subdues the fire in purple Ox, making her less action-oriented than other signs born during a fire year. Yet the water influence makes purple Ox a bit more apt to change than other Oxen. Still, purple Ox would rather boast and act belligerently when faced with changes or challenges.

Purple Ox's personality is direct. She knows what she wants and how to get it. Purple Ox tends to make offensive comments too quickly and too emphatically, hurts others' feelings, and does not think before speaking. When unable to express emotions, purple Ox can become too frank, bold, and coldhearted and cruel to rivals, even devastating in her cruelty.

Like all Oxen, purple Ox is trustworthy and will not lie, steal, or cheat her way to success. But she can feel anger and jealousy toward those who do. Purple Ox wants loved ones to benefit from her success and social status. Purple Ox will sacrifice for family.

Purple Ox finds true success—happiness and joy—through warmhearted generosity. Experiences that are fun, joyful, loving, and pleasurable should be pursued by purple Ox.

土牛 GOLD OX—1949, 2009

Gold Ox is the earth Ox. A valley symbolizes earth's feminine yin energy. If you were born in the year of the gold Ox, a lush valley is where you will be content.

Extreme good fortune blesses the one born in a gold year. The golden one is guarded, safe, and protected, always finding food and shelter. Even strangers will help gold Ox. Gold types will always have life's necessities.

Earth qualities perfectly suit Ox's temperament: stability, honesty, practicality, industry, prudence, reliability, kindness, and loyalty (see page 20). Gold Oxen do well to meditate and contemplate and to nurture themselves physically, emotionally, and spiritually.

Ox's earthly branch is water (see page 22). Water conflicts with the element earth because earth blocks water. Sometimes gold Ox is blocked from expressing her true nature and is less creative. But gold Ox soberly realizes her limitations and does not strive to be the very best.

Gold Ox is not attracted to wild schemes and unknown risks. She is not quick enough for game playing. Instead, gold Ox prefers practical endeavors and seeks the security and stability that wild schemes can't offer.

The water branch gives gold Ox much empathy, caring, and nurturing qualities. The earth year inclines gold Ox to be kind and loyal and to value friendships. She is not a fair-weather friend and will not abandon relationships when fortunes change. Gold Ox is a sensitive, emotional, and understanding partner who is sincere, faithful, and firmly committed in relationships.

When gold Oxen apply themselves they are deserving of their hard-won rewards. Because the golden one is basically fortunate, gold Ox doesn't need to work too hard. Like other Oxen, when focused on a project she will blindly pursue it to completion, but unlike other Oxen, she can be a procrastinator, often delaying action until a circumstance becomes an emergency.

Gold Ox dislikes change and is slow to change. She does not complain, whine, or seek shortcuts. Gold Ox succeeds by demonstrating a sympathetic nature and showing great kindness to others.

金牛 SILVER OX—1901, 1961

Silver Ox is the metal Ox. When metal expresses feminine yin energy, it is symbolized by a kettle. If you were born in the year of the silver Ox, a kettle or cauldron is your personal symbol.

Metal qualities are righteousness, independence, strong will, intensity, uprightness, determination, and ability to focus (see page 21). Many of these are naturally Ox traits, especially righteousness, strong will, intensity, and determination. Silver Ox is the strongest of all Oxen.

Ox's earthly branch is water (see page 22). Water is nurtured by metal because a metal container carries water. Therefore, silver Ox can express herself powerfully, know herself well, and understand her inner nature. Silver Ox is not afraid to tell the truth and intensely express a viewpoint. Unfortunately, sensitivity to others' feelings is not silver Ox's forte, and others may feel overwhelmed and trampled.

Silver Ox is responsible and reliable and fulfills commitments. She can become maniacal when pursuing a goal or committing to a cause. Nothing can stop the silver Ox once dedicated, and woe be to anyone who gets in her way. Silver Ox must not allow iron will and myopic focus to manifest as ruthlessness, cruelty, selfishness, aggressiveness, or argumentative behavior. Metal can retaliate with a vengeance, and silver Ox's rival will find a formidable, intelligent foe. Of all Oxen, silver Ox can work the hardest and feels she deserves the biggest reward for such tireless devotion.

Silver Ox can become stubborn and upset if she cannot dominate a situation, especially in relationships. This Ox rarely accepts responsibility for her contributions to relationship problems. Silver Ox can create unbalanced partnerships of codependence in which she is too controlling of her mate. Silver Ox does well to allow a partner some independence and to not be stubborn or selfish and always wanting her own way. If a divorce occurs, expect silver Ox to provide as little financial support as possible as a revenge tactic and to carry a grudge indefinitely.

A balanced silver Ox is fair and patient. Silver Ox should strive to be less opinionated, accept change, and release the past. The silver Ox finds healing by constructively expressing emotions.

水牛 GRAY OX—1913, 1973

Gray Ox is the water Ox. When it expresses feminine yin energy, water is symbolized by a brook. If you were born in the year of the gray Ox, your personal symbol is a clear brook.

Water qualities include sensitivity, drive, effectiveness, creativity, and a passion for life and sex. Water types value family and social contacts and have the potential to attract them. Ox values are especially in agreement with water's focus on the family. The other water qualities add zest, zeal, and emotional expressiveness to gray Ox. Ox's earthly branch is of the element water (see page 22). Therefore, gray Ox has a double dose of water qualities.

Gray Ox may be the most emotionally mature of all Oxen. She organizes her activities with patience and does not need to dominate, bully, or rigidly control others. Most open to change, and flexible when in a challenging situation or when working with others, gray Ox is sensitive to the emotions and contributions of coworkers. She can be a team player and respect the methods and wishes of others. But like all Oxen, gray Ox desires stability and security, does not relish change, and will not protest against the prevailing social order.

Gray Ox is determined and excels in a creative arena. Others should encourage this individual to express and develop her water qualities. Gray Ox can accomplish many tasks at once and must avoid a tendency to be frantic or overactive, especially if born in the heat of summer when Ox labors.

Gray Ox is a giving person who feels deeply, a compassionate pillar in times of difficulty. Gray Ox will be cherished by friends and family. She is the most sensitive of all Oxen and least likely to offend others.

Sometimes gray Ox can be shy and wants to stay within the security of home. But gray Ox must venture into the world and interact with others to succeed.

木牛 Blue Ox—1925, 1985

Blue Ox is the wood Ox. The feminine, yin aspect of wood is symbolized by the flexible bamboo that bends gently with the winds. If you were born in the year of the blue Ox, the bamboo tree is your totem.

Boldness, creativity, idealism, imagination, planning, decision making, steadfastness, benevolence, and competitiveness are wood qualities. These characteristics add much drive and focus to blue Ox who easily achieves goals (see page 24). Blue Ox's impatient nature enables her to compete, working harder and achieving success more quickly than colleagues.

Ox's earthly branch is water, which helps wood to grow (see page 22). Blue Ox is a lifelong learner who finds happiness and contentment in old age. Blue Ox is intelligent and creative, and possesses many talents and abilities. Because the flexible bamboo tree is her symbol, blue Ox can more easily accept change than other Oxen. She adapts when necessary and is less stern, demanding, and controlling. Blue Ox can be a team player who respects the contributions of others.

Like all Oxen, blue Ox is concerned with issues of stability and security, possesses high scruples, and is honest. The wood birth year gives blue Ox a drive and ambition that is well coupled with the Ox trait of being a steady, reliable worker and partner.

At times, blue Ox can be angry, stubborn, prejudiced, and relentless. Blue Ox does well to remember the bamboo tree and try
to bend with prevailing winds by tempering her competitive tendencies. A balanced blue Ox is flexible and open-minded and chan-
nels anger in constructive ways. She must not repress negative
energy, but should learn to redirect it.

TIGER

*Key words: Vigor, leadership,
courage.
Tiger correlates to the Western sign
Aquarius.*

TIGER LUNAR CALENDAR

1902—February 8 to January 28, 1903	Black Tiger
1914—January 26 to February 13, 1915	Green Tiger
1926—February 13 to January 1, 1927	Red Tiger
1938—January 31 to February 18, 1939	Yellow Tiger
1950—February 17 to February 5, 1951	White Tiger
1962—February 5 to January 24, 1963	Black Tiger
1974—January 23 to February 10, 1975	Green Tiger
1986—February 9 to January 28, 1987	Red Tiger
1998—January 28 to February 15, 1999	Yellow Tiger
2010—February 14 to February 2, 2011	White Tiger
2022—February 1 to January 21, 2023	Black Tiger

TIGER YEAR

Tiger is grand, daring, and powerful. Four mighty Tigers guard
the four directions. North is guarded by the black (water) Tiger
who represents winter. East is guarded by the green (wood)
Tiger who represents spring. South is guarded by the red (fire)
Tiger who represents summer. West is guarded by the white

(metal) Tiger who represents autumn. The center is guarded by the yellow (earth) Tiger who represents the sun.

The Chinese god of wealth, Hsai Shen, rides a tiger, for Tiger brings good fortune. All Tigers scare off thieves, ghosts, and fires. Therefore, Tiger is a formidable animal totem to contact in the shamanic realm to assist in banishments and purifications.

The year of the Tiger is explosive, wildly creative, big, and bold. All of life's activities will be experienced on a grand scale. It is a time of extremes—tempers flare, drama and excitement reign, and crazy dreams can become reality. Expect massive social change, political rebellions, and military coups.

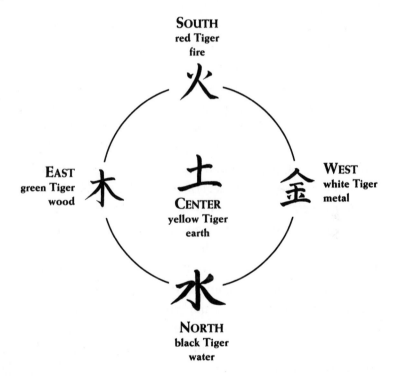

TIGER PERSONALITY

Tiger the hunter is more powerful than a lion. Tiger, not lion, is the king of beasts. A person born in the year of the Tiger has a regal quality and assumes a leadership role whenever possible.

Known for power, determination, and charisma, Tiger aims high and pursues goals with vigor, passion, and daring.

Once Tiger makes a promise or declaration, you can count on him to deliver it. No matter how many obstacles lie in Tiger's path, his courage will not diminish. Tiger attacks targets with unique swiftness and stealth. His actions show a combination of style and power. Tiger stands out in a crowd, a free thinker who never conforms.

On the surface, Tiger is at a loss to engage in conversation and sometimes can appear shy. That is because he is more comfortable being a loner. Tiger is not a team player because he wants things done his way. If Tiger cannot be the leader, he becomes a loner so that his freedom won't be restrained by others. But this loner attitude and pride sometimes prevents Tiger from seeking other people's assistance when faced with an endeavor that calls for someone else's resources and talents.

Despite the iron appearance Tiger puts out to the world, he is quite emotional and sensitive. In the realm of romance, the Tiger male is more practical than the Tiger female, but don't be surprised if Tiger showers a lover with poetry and personal gifts. The Tiger woman loves to be pursued and pampered. She is immensely romantic and demands a great deal of attention from her lovers. She has many expectations of her partners, which can cause difficulties. Tigers want to dominate relationships because of their independent nature and desire to rule.

In traditional Asian cultures, Tiger sons are desired because they are strong, courageous, and daring. Tiger daughters are not preferred because they are considered to be obstinate and headstrong, even abandoning relationships that are not to their liking. A female Tiger won't submit willingly to the Confucian ideal of womanhood, which dictates that a daughter obey her father, a wife obey her husband, and an older woman obey her eldest son.

Tiger can make a great friend for people who appreciate honesty and directness. He doesn't mince words. At times Tiger's temper is difficult to handle. Tiger's negative traits are a tendency to be impulsive, rebellious, and quick tempered. When Tiger throws a tantrum, this anger can spread to innocent bystanders. Tiger often jumps into action too hastily. He needs to learn to stop and think before acting.

TIGER RELATIONSHIPS

Tiger with Rat: Cynical Rat is not impressed with mighty Tiger, whom Rat finds immature and restless. Both are competitive and social, and value success. But together they bring out each other's poorer qualities. In a relationship, impulsive Tiger overspends Rat's hard-earned finances. Industrious Rat resents Tiger's high-maintenance demands and lack of restraint.

Tiger with Ox: Tiger may be attracted to Ox's stability, but disciplined Ox may not appreciate the unpredictable creativity of Tiger. Ox wants to control Tiger, but all attempts will lead to frustration. Tiger soon becomes bored and refuses to obey Ox's strict rules. If these two powerful personalities fight, Ox will win.

Tiger with Tiger: Two independent Tigers need room to roam. They may have to compromise and not be too harsh, stubborn, or demanding with each other. It is advisable for them to budget their finances carefully, since both can be big spenders. Together they possess similar ideals, common values, and lofty goals.

Tiger with Hare: Gentle Hare is attracted to daring, dynamic Tiger. But Tiger may find Hare a bit too conservative or weak, although Tiger does enjoy Hare's intelligence, esthetics, and flattering attention. Tiger needs to be more patient and kind to Hare, who is intimidated by Tiger's strength.

Tiger with Dragon: A classic yin–yang image shows Tiger balanced with Dragon, for Dragon represents the sky and Tiger represents the earth. Dragon brings much-needed wisdom to Tiger, who respects and heeds Dragon's council. But this union could result in an intense power struggle. If they become comrades in arms rather than rivals, there is potential for friendship.

Tiger with Serpent: Elusive Serpent is physically attractive to Tiger. After Tiger enjoys the pursuit, he may discover that they are incompatible. Tiger cannot fully trust suspicious Serpent.

When Serpent is possessive or controlling, Tiger finds such affections suffocating. Tiger and Serpent have very different perspectives on life.

Tiger with Horse: A perfect camaraderie exists between Tiger and Horse. They are both entertaining, independent, freedom loving, lively, creative, and impulsive. Over time, they can sustain their initial sexual attraction. Both share common interests, values, and aspirations. Each allows the other freedom and independence and neither is possessive. Both appreciate direct, frank communications.

Tiger with Sheep: Compassionate Sheep respects Tiger's idealism and lofty goals. Tiger enjoys Sheep's attentive devotion and inspired creativity. But Tiger must adjust to and accept Sheep's fragile and possessive nature. In this combination, Sheep benefits from Tiger's influence.

Tiger with Monkey: Monkey may be the worst possible mate for Tiger. Monkey's wild antics and thirst for attention oppose Tiger's desire to have his own way. They compete with each other, and both refuse to compromise. Monkey antagonizes Tiger, finds his weaknesses, and pulls Tiger's tail. Tiger retaliates in anger by pulling Monkey's tail. Neither can win and both are bad losers. Avoid Monkey, who is Tiger's opposite.

Tiger with Phoenix: Tiger squanders, Phoenix saves. Rebellious Tiger defies Phoenix's need to control, especially their mutual finances. Together their blunt style of communicating can become very negative when they argue. Critical Phoenix finds fault with Tiger's flamboyant lifestyle, emotional reactions, and lack of attention to detail. Phoenix barely tolerates Tiger's unconventional methods and large ego. Tiger's many positive characteristics aren't appreciated in this combination.

Tiger with Dog: Dog is an excellent marriage or business partner for Tiger. Dog respects Tiger's idealism and allows Tiger some privacy. Tiger appreciates Dog's loyalty and helpfulness. When Tiger becomes too hotheaded, Dog offers valuable common-sense advice. They possess similar goals and appreciate their shared affection. Tiger and Dog can create a very sympathetic bond of mutual understanding.

Tiger with Boar: Tiger finds a strong ally in the kind affectionate Boar. Tiger admires Boar's stamina, courage, and good nature. Boar admires Tiger's idealism and joy in life. Sexually, they are very compatible; Tiger's passion unites with Boar's sensuality. They can combine forces to achieve common goals. Together they can enjoy life and find happiness.

TIGER CHILD AND PARENT

The Tiger child is a ball of energy! A hyperactive chatterbox, he will pounce on new opportunities. A Tiger cub freely expresses emotions, so it is not difficult to figure him out. The Tiger child requires discipline combined with much love and warmth, as well as constant creative stimuli. Care must be taken to teach the child to share and not bully smaller children. Night-born Tigers are more fortunate, since these big cats are nocturnal hunters. A Tiger born close to midnight is most lucky. A Tiger born after sunrise, especially close to noon, may encounter more obstacles to financial success.

The Tiger parent is a despotic ruler at home. Children are expected to obey and show respect. Tiger parents' decisions will supersede a child's wishes. Arguing with the powerful Tiger is not an option. Tiger parents have high expectations for their offspring. The same rules of compatibility apply as for Tiger relationships: Tiger parents favor Horse, Dog, and Boar children who gleefully do as they demand. Tiger, Hare, Dragon, and Sheep children learn quickly to follow Tiger rules and comply. But Rat, Ox, Serpent, Monkey, and Phoenix children may try to rebel or express individuality—but to no avail. All must do as Tiger decrees.

TIGER IN THE TWELVE-BRANCH CYCLE

Tiger in Rat year: Expect minimal gains and advancements. Restless Tiger requires action, but money is tight and compromises must be accepted.

Tiger in Ox year: This time brings frustration because Ox influence requires Tiger to work hard and become serious. Advantage can be had if Tiger controls his temper and doesn't rebel. This is not an advantageous time to start new endeavors.

Tiger in Tiger year: Expect good fortune, luck, recognition, protection, and benevolence. Tiger is empowered by experiencing his own year, but should refrain from overspending.

Tiger in Hare year: Expect a happy, easy year of rest and relaxation in which personal affairs will run smoothly, business can be successful, and goals may be attained.

Tiger in Dragon year: Dragon's dynamic energy will stimulate Tiger and bring excitement and diverse activities. Tiger does best to compromise should difficult situations arise.

Tiger in Serpent year: Expect opportunities for healing and creating balance after the wild Dragon year. Travel is highlighted and this year is an outstanding time for a relaxing vacation.

Tiger in Horse year: Expect excellent fortune, happiness, and no danger. Horse is Tiger's friend (as is Dog). This may be one of the best years of the twelve-branch cycle.

Tiger in Sheep year: Expect a quieter year when Tiger does best to focus attention on home and family. A Sheep year is favorable for relaxing travel and culinary enjoyment.

Tiger in Monkey year: Prepare for the most uncomfortable year
in the twelve-branch cycle because Monkey is Tiger's rival. Most
endeavors will lead to disappointments. Not a favorable year
for marriage.

Tiger in Phoenix year: Expect minor disappointments and some
unhappiness as Tiger recovers from a Monkey year. Friends,
family, and colleagues will offer their support.

Tiger in Dog year: Expect an excellent year because Dog is Tiger's
friend (as is Horse). Tiger may find devotion to a cause. Work
is successful with good investments and fortunate enterprise.

Tiger in Boar year: Expect good business, wild luck, happiness,
and contentment. Boar is Tiger's dear friend, so Boar's influence brings enjoyment of the finer things in life, but don't overspend or overextend.

火 RED TIGER—1926, 1986
虎

Red Tiger is the fire Tiger. If you were born in the year of
the red Tiger, burning wood, which symbolizes fire's masculine yang energy, is your creative symbol.

Fire qualities are reason, expressiveness, spirituality, intuition,
insight, dynamism, passion, aggressiveness, leadership, and refinement (see page 18). These creative qualities add desirable traits to
Tiger's character. Direct red Tiger has little problem with self-
expression.

Red Tiger is not a weak soul. He possesses great energy, enthusiasm, creativity, and energy. Unpredictable and always moving,
red Tiger loves travel, excitement, challenges, and danger. He is
daring and independent, and desires action, passion, and a large
stage on which to perform. Red Tiger is a natural entertainer and
powerful orator, yearning to influence others and demanding to
be noticed. His life is experienced on a grand scale.

Red Tiger is a leader. No one can tell him what to do or how to
do it. He follows the dictates of his own heart, no matter how
wild, far fetched, or impractical the goals may be. Red Tigers will
not compromise nor let anyone or anything stand in their way.

These ambitious nonconformists will do as they please with little regard for those who disagree.

Red Tiger can have a violent temper, exploding if affairs do not go according to his timetable. This can be very upsetting to calmer and more gentle coworkers and family members (such as Hare, Sheep, and Boar), who justifiably fear red Tiger's wrath.

Tiger's earthly branch is the element wood (see page 24). Wood feeds fire, so red Tiger is endlessly supplied with the energy necessary to complete extreme endeavors and wild schemes. Red Tiger will succeed through sheer willpower, drive, and courage.

Balanced fire gives red Tiger a sense of justice and restraint; this is the rare Tiger who knows when to stop. Red Tiger succeeds by developing warmhearted generosity. Fun, joyful, loving, and pleasurable experiences should be pursued by red Tiger.

土 Yellow Tiger—1938, 1998

虎 Yellow Tiger is the earth Tiger. When earth symbolizes masculine yang energy, it is symbolized by a hill. If you were born in the year of the yellow Tiger, a hill or mountain is your personal symbol.

Earth qualities include stability, honesty, practicality, industry, prudence, reliability, kindness, and loyalty (see page 20). These qualities enrich yellow Tiger's character and add needed stability. Only the yellow Tiger is a practical, levelheaded, and responsible Tiger due to the earth influence. Yellow Tiger is less likely to manipulate others to succeed, or to lash out with an uncontrollable temper.

Yellow Tiger has the potential to be a well-rounded and mature individual without losing any of Tiger's innate curiosity and creativity. He is thoughtful, intelligent, and able to plan endeavors without having to rush in blindly and later be forced to accept the consequences. Able to balance intense passions, yellow Tiger will succeed admirably by applying that Tiger energy and enthusiasm to many projects and following through to completion. He is less rebellious than other Tigers and will not sabotage opportunities.

Empathetic yellow Tiger can be a kind, compassionate soul

who understands others, is sensitive to their needs, and values their contributions. He possesses a keen awareness of the emotional reactions of others and tries to be helpful. In business, yellow Tiger respects the methodologies of coworkers and peers without having to be the center of attention. He is pragmatic and realistic in relationships, unlike others Tigers whose relationships are often based on lust and fantasy. Yet like all Tigers, yellow Tiger can be unwittingly self-absorbed.

Tiger's earthly branch is wood (see page 24). Earth nurtures wood, which slows down the impatient Tiger and helps him to evolve his spiritual side. Yellow Tiger should spend time meditating and attend to his physical, emotional, and spiritual well-being. Balanced earth makes yellow Tiger reliable, sincere, and faithful. Yellow Tiger succeeds by being sympathetic and kind to others.

金虎 WHITE TIGER—1950, 2010

White Tiger is the metal Tiger. When metal expresses masculine yang energy, it is symbolized by a weapon, the personal symbol of anyone born in the year of the white Tiger.

Righteousness, independence, strong will, intensity, uprightness, determination, and the ability to focus are both metal qualities and natural Tiger characteristics (see page 21). That is why the regal white Tiger may be the most powerful animal of the Taoist zodiac.

White Tiger is a powerful leader and self-starter, a lustful warrior who loves freedom and desires complete artistic control and full self-expression. He is a fearless soul who demands attention and admiration for his bravery and passionate nature.

White Tiger works relentlessly to achieve a goal, but only if it is a cause or project in which he sincerely believes. Impatient with the frailties of others, white Tiger achieves results where others cannot, even though the methodologies are often unconventional, daring, and not well planned. When challenged, white Tiger can become unnecessarily aggressive and argumentative, especially if asked to restrain himself or made to conform.

In relationships, white Tiger (especially a female white Tiger) can contribute to codependent partnerships in which white Tiger is too demanding. White Tiger does well to not be stubborn and selfish, and to allow mates some independence. White Tiger's mate can benefit greatly by having such a strong partner.

Wood is the earthly branch of Tiger (see page 24). Wood has an antagonistic relationship to metal because metal cuts wood. This can inhibit the emotional and intellectual development of white Tiger. In some instances, the metal nature can be cutting and result in a dual personality with much inner conflict. In order to best integrate the metal and wood elements, white Tiger needs to slow down and not become overwhelmed. Otherwise, he can inadvertently make social blunders when refusing to deal with internal issues.

Balanced metal makes white Tiger fair and patient. He succeeds by being less opinionated, accepting change, and gracefully releasing the past instead of seeking revenge. White Tiger's challenge is to learn how to express emotions, including grief, and to find his own way of healing.

水虎 BLACK TIGER—1902, 1962

Black Tiger is the water Tiger. When water expresses masculine yang energy it is symbolized by a wave. If you were born in the year of the black Tiger, your personal symbol is a cresting wave.

Sensitivity, drive, effectiveness, creativity, and passion for life and sex are water qualities (see page 22). Water is the most yin element, balancing Tiger's aggressiveness. According to the Taoists, water's power lies in its ability to surround any obstacle without compromising its essential nature.

Black Tiger is a lucky, open-minded, and intuitive individual who can create a harmonious and successful life. Water calms black Tiger and helps him intelligently express powerfully felt ideals. Mentally quick and astute, he can assess situations correctly and behave accordingly. Black Tiger is less impractical, unrealistic, temperamental, and selfish than other Tigers. A mature black Tiger possesses emotional balance, patience, and clarity of purpose.

Tiger's earthly branch is the element wood (see page 24). Water feeds wood and helps wood to grow. Black Tiger is sensitive, caring, and nurturing toward others because he knows how to take care of himself.

Black Tiger sometimes experiences difficulties in relationships because water succeeds by attracting, not pursuing. Tiger would rather be the hunter and pursue. The earthly branch wood makes all Tigers impatient, but black Tiger benefits by biding his time and waiting for the most opportune moment to engage in a relationship.

Black Tiger must strive to be brave and not allow sentiment or fear to block the fullest expression of creativity. If overwhelmed, black Tiger can be frantic or overactive, especially if he was born at night when Tiger hunts. Black Tiger's challenge is to overcome fear and become an active participant in life.

木 虎 GREEN TIGER—1914, 1974

Green Tiger is the wood Tiger. When wood expresses masculine yang energy, it is symbolized by a sturdy and upright pine tree. Those born in the year of the green Tiger have the pine as a personal symbol.

Wood qualities include boldness, creativity, idealism, imagination, and competitiveness. These traits are expressed strongly by green Tiger, who stands out in a crowd and is always noticed. He is true to himself and does only as he pleases.

Tiger's earthly branch is wood (see page 24). Green Tiger has a double dose of wood's growth and enthusiasm. He is highly creative, imaginative, and benevolent, eagerly embraces new projects, and is well loved and admired by many. Green Tiger is lucky in love, social, popular, and always in the know. Dynamic green Tiger is a winner who easily achieves goals, and experiences much growth throughout life.

Green Tiger seeks fun and avoids discipline. Disliking hard work, green Tiger prefers an easier route. Often too impatient to complete what he has begun, he would rather delegate work and then accept praise for a job well done by others. If circumstances or people prove too difficult, green Tiger will move on to other opportunities. When this keenly aware Tiger senses a losing competition, he will promptly exit, knowing that a new batch of friends, partners, and supporters is not far away. It is easier for resourceful green Tiger to create new projects than to fix what needs repairing.

Like all Tigers, green Tiger will not accept rules and criticism. If challenged, he can become stubborn, angry, and prejudiced. Balanced wood makes green Tiger flexible and open-minded. Green Tiger must learn to control anger and competitiveness and redirect this energy into positive actions.

HARE

Key words: Friendliness, diplomacy, adaptability. Hare correlates to the Western sign Pisces.

HARE LUNAR CALENDAR

1903—January 29 to February 15, 1904 Gray Hare
1915—February 14 to February 2, 1916 Blue Hare
1927—February 2 to January 22, 1928 Purple Hare
1939—February 19 to February 7, 1940 Gold Hare
1951—February 6 to January 26, 1952 Silver Hare
1963—January 25 to February 12, 1964 Gray Hare
1975—February 11 to January 30, 1976 Blue Hare
1987—January 29 to February 16, 1988 Purple Hare
1999—February 16 to February 4, 2000 Gold Hare
2011—February 3 to January 22, 2012 Silver Hare
2023—January 22 to February 9, 2024 Gray Hare

HARE YEAR

The legend of the moon goddess Ch'ang-o is associated with the Hare. Ch'ang-o was the wife of an archer named Ki. Brave Ki shot down ten suns when the suns rose together to scorch the earth. Although Ki was courageous, he was a ruthless man. In reward for shooting the suns, Ki was given a brew of immortality. One day when her husband was out hunting, Ch'ang-o drank this brew in an attempt to stop his cruelty. When Ki returned and realized what had happened, he tried to kill Ch'ang-o, but she escaped to the moon and was protected by the moon Hare. Afraid to return to earth, Ch'ang-o lived happily with the moon Hare and became a moon goddess and protector of children. Hare's lunar connection is that it takes 28 days, one lunar month, before newborn Hares are ready to leave their mothers.

Translations occasionally render Hare as Cat or Rabbit (do not confuse Cat with Tiger, who has very different attributes). Hares differ slightly from rabbits in that rabbits are born naked and blind, whereas hares are born with a coat of fur and good vision. Hares run faster than rabbits and do not freeze when confronted by danger. Hares symbolize long life, as do cranes and turtles.

The year of the Hare is a time of peace, calm, leisure, and rest after the chaos of the previous Tiger year. People enjoy the arts, gourmet food, and luxuries. Money can be made easily, but it is spent easily. The Dragon year that follows will be a wild and exhausting time, so enjoy a Hare year as an opportunity for relaxation, pleasure, family gatherings, entertainment, and comfortable travel. Expect political compromise and diplomatic peacemaking on a global level.

Hare Personality

The person born in a Hare year is even-tempered, well-mannered, amiable, friendly, sensitive, and artistic. Hare's diplomatic ability makes her welcome in social circles. Hare longs for companionship and dislikes being alone, so she adapts easily to any environment and makes every effort to conform. Hare is keenly perceptive and can sense danger in any situation. She quickly takes action to protect herself. An old Chinese proverb says, "A swift Hare has three holes," meaning that the smart Hare has three holes dug in the ground, ready to escape through any one of them whenever a predator approaches. Hare is not a fighter; she would rather flee than confront conflicts.

Hare's peaceful nature makes her a great team player who rarely pursues personal glory at the expense of peers. Hare doesn't want to make enemies and goes out of her way to avoid arguments and conflicts. Hare strives to create a harmonious work and social environment where she is comfortable.

On the other hand, a fear of conflict can make Hare wishy-washy, indecisive, secretive, edgy, or even paranoid. She sometimes finds it difficult to voice opinions in public, especially when the ideas are unconventional. Hare prefers not to fight for social or political causes and is content to enjoy the peace and quiet of the little circle Hare creates for herself.

Hare pays much attention to her appearances and manners. She is usually very conservative and dislikes taking risks. Though Hare's lifestyle is usually pleasant, pursuing breakthroughs and transformations are not Hare goals. Instead, she prefers peace, security, and beauty. Hare excels in the arts, and Hare's sense of aesthetics and beauty can be parlayed into a successful career. Hare can become a prosperous painter, musician, or designer.

When it comes to affairs of the heart, both male and female Hares are extremely romantic. The female Hare is gentle and sensitive, enjoying romantic walks by the ocean under starlight. Lady Hare likes cosmetics and fancy costumes. Male Hare is gallant and sensitive. Though he may be conservative when faced with challenges, he has no problem with equality in relationships. He doesn't mind cooking, cleaning, and decorating the house. Regardless of gender, Hare rarely fights or competes with a partner.

HARE RELATIONSHIPS

Hare with Rat: Diplomatic Hare and charming Rat both know how to please. But they have different financial values. Industrious Rat hoards hard-earned money; Hare would rather indulge on luxuries and finery. Hare may have to compromise because Rat will not lower her expectations. Together they can share intimate emotions and create a lovely home.

Hare with Ox: Reliable Ox can offer Hare the reassurance, security, and stability that helps Hare to succeed. Kind and

emotional Hare can understand Ox's difficulties and sympathize with Ox's burdens. But Hare may have to follow Ox's orders and not become upset if Ox is stern and critical. If Hare can toughen up and not become bored with Ox predictability, their relationship will improve with time.

Hare with Tiger: Although Hare may be attracted to dynamic Tiger, Tiger may not respect Hare in return. Tiger has no desire to adjust her extreme temperament to match peaceful Hare. Tiger's independence and boldness may cause stress for security-seeking Hare. Hare may be eaten alive after much sacrifice and martyrdom.

Hare with Hare: Two Hares are artistic, gentle, and quiet souls who value peace and harmony. Socially, they enjoy tasteful parties and elegant celebrations. They share mutual interests in fashion, home decoration, fine cuisine, and the collecting of fine objects. Their lovely home will be a creative environment. They are affectionate and courteous with each other. This relationship is especially compatible between two men.

Hare with Dragon: There may be a strong initial physical attraction between these two sensuous signs. Both love celebration, merriment, and excitement, and enjoy each other's company. Hare's fine sense of diplomacy and intelligence can be assets that further Dragon's ambitions. Dragon is powerful enough to offer Hare security and make decisions when Hare vacillates. But Dragon's chaotic life, full of fireworks, may be overwhelming to nervous Hare, who prefers a smoother path in relationships.

Hare with Serpent: Together these two intelligent, cultivated, and creative signs share a love of the arts, literature, and theater. Hare domesticates Serpent by offering a beautiful environment. But problems could develop if Serpent is too possessive or controlling. Hare must be firm, speak up, and not allow herself to be dominated.

Hare with Horse: Hare may not take Horse seriously because rash Horse may be too unreliable, unstable, and untamable for Hare. Horse will not adjust her extreme temperament to match gentle Hare. Hare may find Horse selfish and unwittingly cruel. Hare may experience similar emotional problems as with Tiger, Horse's best friend.

Hare with Sheep: Both possess the soul of an artist with identical values of loving peace, calm, and harmony in all things. Together they can enjoy romance, mutual kindness, and an almost telepathic way of communicating. They share exquisite tastes and a love of refined surroundings, and both spend lavishly. These two signs crave security, and together create shelter and protection from the coarse world.

Hare with Monkey: Unpredictable Monkey cannot offer Hare much-desired security. Restless Monkey may feel restrained by Hare's cloying domesticity. Hare does not know whether to trust Monkey, who easily can trick gullible Hare. Monkey craves attention and thrives on controversy. All this is upsetting to Hare, who has little to gain in this partnership.

Hare with Phoenix: Phoenix may be the worst possible mate for Hare. Hare spends on luxuries, while Phoenix is obsessive about money. Phoenix's constant looking for battles to fight and wrongs to right is exhausting for peaceful Hare. Hare wants only tranquillity, not endless criticism. Avoid Phoenix, who is Hare's opposite.

Hare with Dog: Hare finds a strong ally in faithful Dog. Hare brings Dog peace, quiet, serenity, and a warm home. Charming Hare forgives Dog's lack of finesse. In return, entertaining Dog forgives Hare's moods and offers security and protection from the demanding world. They bring out the finest qualities in each other and are extremely compatible.

Hare with Boar: Hare brings refinement, intelligence, and social graces to kind Boar. In return Boar brings sympathy, liveliness, and optimism. Boar's devotion and unselfishness offers Hare the security she craves. Both are gentle souls who are noncritical of each other. Together they can create peace and contentment, although spending must be controlled.

HARE CHILD AND PARENT

The Hare child is sweet, good, and kind. She loves animals and possesses a peaceful, gentle soul. Little Hare is a very easy child to raise because she is obedient and quiet, doesn't argue, and is sensitive to parents' difficulties. Such a sensitive child is susceptible to illnesses and may need pampering. Hare children, particularly boys, are often bullied by other children. The Hare child blossoms in an environment of peace, security, and a small safe room or outdoor area for creative play. Enroll Hare children in art, drama, or dance classes (regardless of gender) where they will excel. The Hare child is happier and calmer if born in the summer when life is easier. The Hare born in the cold of winter, when Hare must struggle to survive, may at times be overactive or prone to melancholia.

Many cultures consider Hare to be a fertility symbol. Ironically, people born in a Hare year prefer small families with only one or two children. The calamity and chaos that children bring are disruptive to calm Hare. Therefore, Hares are not the most attentive parents. The Hare parent teaches etiquette to her offspring and demands good manners. The same rules of compatibility apply as for Hare relationships: Hare favors Sheep, Boar, and Dog children. Sheep and Boar children are secure in a quiet, peaceful home. Sheep enjoys the prissy artifice of perfect table manners.

Dog wants to please and can be trained easily to obey. Hare is basically compatible with Rat, Ox, another Hare, Dragon, and Serpent children. All can benefit from learning Hare protocol, although a Dragon child may be a bit testy. But Tiger, Horse, Monkey, and Phoenix children may be trying for the Hare parent. Tiger, Horse, and Monkey play too roughly and are loud. Crowing Phoenix will not be silenced. Hare parents may respond by withdrawing from the child.

HARE IN THE TWELVE-BRANCH CYCLE

Hare in Rat year: Expect a good year with opportunities for advancement. An auspicious time to change residence or invest in real estate. Work progresses steadily, but examine all documents carefully and be less naively trusting.

Hare in Ox year: Expect some difficulties due to unrealistic standards from others. Hare may experience feelings of frustration because rewards are delayed or projects take much longer than anticipated. Not an auspicious time to move. Hare survives unharmed.

Hare in Tiger year: The impulsive and explosive energy of Tiger clashes with Hare's peaceful nature. Unplanned changes and too much excitement can make Hare nervous. Stay calm and conserve energy.

Hare in Hare year: Expect one of the best years in the entire twelve-branch cycle. Hare is greatly empowered by experiencing her own year. People are harmonious, pleasing, and congenial. Opportunities abound, success is inevitable, and family life is very rich.

Hare in Dragon year: Expect much activity and movement, which can be to Hare's benefit if she is motivated and maintains an optimistic attitude. New friends and acquaintances can prove beneficial. If too overextended, retreat and rest at home.

Hare in Serpent year: Expect an uneven time when Hare may be forced to change residence or occupation. Unexpected surprises may occur, which endanger Hare's love of peace and tranquillity. Hare does best by remaining neutral and not getting too wrapped up in Serpent's coils.

Hare in Horse year: Expect a better year and a chance to recover from the previous Serpent year's difficulties. Romance, travel, social enjoyment, and pleasant surprises (especially in relationships) are foreseen.

Hare in Sheep year: Expect a wonderful year because Sheep is Hare's best friend. Events flow smoothly and Hare has many opportunities to indulge her fine tastes. Hare possesses the ability to transcend difficulties.

Hare in Monkey year: Expect a smoother year than one might anticipate in wild Monkey time. Hare enjoys festive social events and exotic entertainment. Try to rest if overstimulated.

Hare in Phoenix year: Expect difficulties because Phoenix is Hare's foe. A difficult year, especially financially. Monetary strain can bring debt. Hard work is foreseen, causing frustration and anger. The general martial tone of the Phoenix influence irritates Hare's fine sensibilities.

Hare in Dog year: Expect a pleasant year because Dog is Hare's friend and defender. Recovery from the previous Phoenix year's difficulties is foreseen, but career still requires attention. Hare benefits by playing political angles and being diplomatic.

Hare in Boar year: Expect a nice year because Boar is compatible with Hare. A year to enjoy the good times, emotional security, and social contentment. But keep expectations low because accomplishments may be negligible.

火 兔 Purple Hare—1927, 1987

Purple Hare is the fire Hare. Fire expressing feminine yin energy is symbolized by the flame of a lamp. If you were born in the year of the purple Hare, a pure flame is your personal symbol for meditation.

Fire qualities—reason, expressiveness, spirituality, intuition, insight, dynamism, passion, aggressiveness, leadership, and good manners—add power and decisiveness to purple Hare's personality (see page 18). She is the most aggressive and action-oriented Hare, one of the strongest of these otherwise timid souls.

Since a proper sense of etiquette is a specific Hare tendency as well as a fire trait, purple Hare can be the most cordial and well-behaved of all the fire signs. The fire traits of anger and emotional outbursts are controlled and tempered due to Hare's innate reserve and diplomatic qualities. Purple Hare will not aggressively confront others. Instead, she would rather put people at ease.

Purple Hare can be a leader, unlike other Hares, because people trust her. She will curry favor and promote her own interests but with such arresting charm and innocence that others will be swayed. Purple Hare benefits by surrounding herself with positive and supportive companions and coworkers. Considerate and appreciative comrades help her to succeed.

Purple Hare expresses emotions well and is in touch with her feelings. A true believer, she is often psychic and succeeds by following intuitive hunches. She is receptive to the feelings of others and is a soothing counselor in others' times of trouble. Sensitive purple Hare is extremely receptive to the stimulus of environment and dislikes unpleasant surroundings, loud noises, or chaos.

Like all fire signs, purple Hare can be extremely emotional. She benefits by staying grounded and centered, and not indulging in irrational dramas or impulsive extremes. Experiences that are fun, joyful, loving, and pleasurable are to be pursued by purple Hare.

The fiery nature is expressed easily by purple Hare. This is because Hare's earthly branch is the element wood (see page 24). Wood feeds fire, enabling purple Hare to meet challenges and attain goals. She has great potential for success, especially if in the company of helpful, mature, and discriminating companions.

 ## GOLD HARE—1939, 1999

Gold Hare is the earth Hare. When expressing feminine yin energy, earth is symbolized by a valley. If you were born in the year of the gold Hare, a lush valley is where you will be most content.

The one born in a gold year is guarded, safe, and protected, blessed by extreme good fortune. A gold sign will always have life's necessities of food and shelter and will enjoy the help of strangers.

Earth qualities are stability, honesty, practicality, industry, prudence, reliability, kindness, and loyalty (see page 20). These characteristics add fortitude to gold Hare's temperament. The earth influence gives gold Hare a sense of direction in life and the groundedness necessary to succeed. Earth also balances Hare's tendency toward emotional excess.

Gold Hare's refined intuition and psychic skills are her best guides in life. She thinks and meditates before acting on plans. More rational and pragmatic than other Hares, she can plan the future realistically by combining psychic insight with earth-plane reality.

Gold Hare, like all Hares, is a sensitive soul who is sympathetic to others. She is an intelligent Hare who is valued by family, friends, and coworkers. This Hare's serious and steadfast ways are appreciated by employers. Gold Hare can make the best of any situation and will strive for material gains. All Hares appreciate fine worldly goods, but the gold Hare's primary concern is material comfort.

Hare's earthly branch is the element wood (see page 24). Wood grows out of the earth and is nurtured by earth. Therefore, gold Hare often finds herself in the role of nurturer or caregiver. For this reason, gold Hare is often successful in a healing profession where a sympathetic nature and natural kindness is appreciated. She may be passionate about work, but is not aggressively active due to a mild, introverted nature.

Gold Hare succeeds by being reliable, sincere, and faithful. She finds happiness by demonstrating sympathy and kindness to others.

SILVER HARE—1951, 2011

Silver Hare is the metal Hare. When it expresses feminine yin energy, metal is symbolized by a kettle or cauldron, the personal symbol of those born in the year of the silver Hare.

Righteousness, independence, strong will, intensity, uprightness, determination, and ability to focus are metal qualities (see page 21). Since these qualities are not natural Hare traits, silver Hare may be the most powerful of all Hares, possessing more courage, conviction, physical strength, and recuperative powers. Only silver Hare can be a leader, self-starter, and boss, unlike other Hares who may lack decisiveness and clarity of purpose.

Silver Hare is a dedicated worker who strives to achieve success. Design, culinary arts, film, photography, and all the fine arts are fields in which silver Hare can become accomplished. She is a well-groomed connoisseur of the finest things in life and wishes to exercise her refined, impeccable tastes. Anyone or anything coarse or vulgar is repulsive to the elegant silver Hare, who is attracted only to beauty.

Most Hares are known for their sympathetic nature, but silver Hare may be the least sympathetic of all Hares. The metal influence makes her more selfish than selfless. She desires money (metal), success, and a lavish lifestyle. She rarely allows her ambitions to be thwarted. Unlike other Hares, silver Hare does not want to compromise and placate the desires of others.

Silver Hare thinks that she is always right, and believes that her keen intuition and insight will never fail. Guided by inner awareness, silver Hare can succeed. She is uncannily gifted in the psychic realm and has much insight into the psychological workings of others.

The earthly branch of Hare is wood (see page 24). Wood has an antagonistic relationship with metal because metal cuts wood. This can inhibit the emotional and intellectual development of silver Hare. In some instances, the cutting metal nature can result in much inner conflict. In order to best integrate the metal and wood elements, silver Hare needs to slow down and not become overwhelmed by materialist ambition. Silver Hare must not indulge in self-pity, dark moods, and the tendency toward a very pessimistic, even fatalistic, outlook. Yet silver Hare rarely burdens others with these irrational fears due to an independent nature and love of privacy.

Silver Hare succeeds by being less opinionated, accepting change, and gracefully releasing the past. Silver Hare's challenge is to learn how to express emotions, including grief, and find her own way of healing.

水 兔 GRAY HARE—1903, 1963

Gray Hare is the water Hare. When water expresses feminine yin energy, it is symbolized by a brook. If you were born in the year of the gray Hare, your personal symbol is a clear brook.

The most yin element, water adds even more softness to the gentle Hare nature in this combination. Water qualities are sensitivity, drive, effectiveness, creativity, and a passion for life and sex. Water types value family and social contacts (see page 22). Water qualities are compatible with Hare's nature. Hare is especially in agreement with the water qualities of sensitivity and creativity.

Gray Hare is one of the most sensitive people of the Taoist zodiac. An extremely deep-feeling and empathetic soul, she dislikes any negative or violent circumstances. Gray Hare should avoid aggressive people and competitive encounters. Instead, she should strive to maintain peace and harmony. A spiritual retreat, monastery, or other peaceful, healing environment is the perfect place for the kind and gentle gray Hare. She is a psychic "sponge" who benefits by absorbing spiritual rather than aggressive vibrations.

If pushed to succeed, sensitive gray Hare can become frantic, especially if born in the cold of winter when Hare must struggle to survive. Fear of a coarse cruel world can make gray Hare shy and timid, always wanting to stay home in the cozy Hare hutch. Therefore, gray Hare must choose the most peaceful work environment in order to excel.

Gray Hare is intelligent and carefully picks her companions. Trustworthy companions can keep gray Hare on the right path. They help when gray Hare indulges in emotional extremes, touchy oversensitivity, even paranoia. Gray Hare is indecisive and constantly vacillates. Others can help gray Hare to maintain a clear perspective and not become clouded by irrational fears and worries.

Hare's earthly branch is the element wood (see page 24). Water feeds wood and helps wood to grow. Gray Hare can attain much emotional growth and spiritual enlightenment in this lifetime. Gray Hare wants others to grow and develop spiritual qualities, too. To achieve this goal, gray Hare nurtures others, easily expressing her mothering or fathering qualities. Family and friends love and cherish the gray Hare and appreciate her kind, helpful, and sympathetic nature. Gray Hares must also remember to nurture themselves, not just others.

BLUE HARE—1915, 1975

Blue Hare is the wood Hare. The feminine, yin aspect of wood energy is symbolized by the flexible bamboo that bends gently with the winds. If you were born in the year of the blue Hare, the bamboo is your tree totem.

Wood qualities—boldness, creativity, idealism, imagination, planning, steadfastness, benevolence, and competitiveness—lend much drive and focus to blue Hare, who can easily achieve goals. Blue Hare has the potential to succeed at any type of undertaking and in any type of environment and is able to initiate and complete new projects.

The earthly branch of Hare is of the wood element (see page 24). Blue Hare has a double dose of wood's action-oriented drive. Unlike other Hares, blue Hare can succeed in business and the corporate realm due to this strong wood influence. She is an active participant in worldly affairs, an inspired and creative soul who wants to achieve and make a mark on the world. Blue Hare is focused and competitive, yet will not abuse others to attain success. Like all Hares, blue Hare possesses the kind, peaceful, and intuitive Hare qualities, and inspires others to develop their potential.

Blue Hare is very generous and understanding, one who enjoys serving and doing for others. Blue Hare must be cautious that others do not take advantage of her good nature, generosity, and kindly sympathetic ways. She must learn to be more discerning when choosing companions and not develop emotional attachments to those who will exploit her.

Blue Hare often lacks direction during youth. She enjoys experimenting in the arts and may become a dilettante. Blue Hare is often a late bloomer who achieves success by middle age and in later life. Old age often finds blue Hare surrounded by comfortable circumstances and fine companions.

DRAGON

Key words: Power, passion, drive. Dragon correlates to the Western sign Aries.

DRAGON LUNAR CALENDAR

1904—February 16 to February 3, 1905   Green Dragon
1916—February 3 to January 22, 1917   Red Dragon
1928—January 23 to February 9, 1929   Yellow Dragon
1940—February 8 to January 26, 1941   White Dragon
1952—January 27 to February 13, 1953   Black Dragon
1964—February 13 to February 1, 1965   Green Dragon
1976—January 31 to February 17, 1977   Red Dragon
1988—February 17 to February 15, 1989 Yellow Dragon
2000—February 5 to January 23, 2001   White Dragon
2012—January 23 to February 9, 2013   Black Dragon
2024—February 10 to January 28, 2025   Green Dragon

DRAGON YEAR

In the West, the Dragon is a hideous beast who symbolizes the worst moral qualities of humanity. According to European medieval legends, brave knights fought Dragons, the foes of virtue. When St. George of Cappadocia, a Roman soldier, slew the Dragon, he killed all that was ugly in Christendom. Dragon was often seen as the devil himself, diabolical Satan, as in this quotation from

Revelations 12:7, "And there was a war in heaven: Michael and his angels fought against the dragon."

In Asian cultures, the qualities of Dragon are the opposite of European interpretations. Dragon is not an evil, malefic enemy. Instead, Dragon symbolizes royalty, prosperity, wisdom, and benevolence. Dragon has magnanimous and spiritual qualities and is a protector of temples and monasteries. Dragon has magical attributes because Dragon can change shape and transform himself into any type of creature.

Dragon brings rain and represents masculine, yang power. In China, the celestial dragon, T'ien Lung, protects the gods and goddesses in heaven. T'ien Lung flies through the sky, chasing the sun.

Dragon is a mythological creature. In ancient times, primordial humanity may have worshiped, or been in awe of, serpents and the sun. The development of the imaginary Dragon fulfilled a role in the psyche of ancient peoples.

The year of the Dragon is a time of ambition, power, and daring. Events seem as if they are magnified threefold with increased intensity. The energy and vitality of the Dragon year may make some people overly optimistic. A Dragon year is an excellent time to start a business, marry, have children, and take incredible risks. On a global level, expect extreme earth changes, such as earthquakes, volcanic eruptions, and tidal waves.

Dragon Personality

Dragon was the most sacred mystical animal throughout thousands of years of Chinese history. Dragon was associated with imperial majesty. For example, the chair on which a Chinese emperor sat was referred to as the "Dragon Chair," and the robe a Chinese emperor wore was called the "Dragon Robe."

A person born in a Dragon year is blessed by the gods and goddesses in heaven. Dragon has strong karma to lead and succeed. This is why during a Dragon year, the population in China increases significantly. A Dragon son is preferred because he will go forth in the world, overcome obstacles, succeed, and return to the family and increase their fortune. A Dragon daughter is not desired because a female Dragon won't submit willingly to the Confucian "three virtues for women" that demand obedience to father, husband and, in old age, eldest son.

Sometimes a Dragon woman is feared by society because she is an independent thinker and strong believer in equal rights. She is not afraid to take charge. Some men find the Dragon woman intimidating because she has a strong personality and possesses abilities that can suppress male peers.

Dragon is full of life, bravery, and intensity. He is a fighter who won't easily allow defeat. Extremely independent and freedom-loving, Dragon needs an environment that allows the liberty to express creativity and nurture personal growth. Passionate and direct Dragon can't tolerate pretentious behavior in people. Run by his heart and emotions, Dragon is often an exquisite lover whose smoldering sexuality attracts many suitors.

A dreamer, Dragon loves adventures and believes that he is destined to achieve great success. Dragon wants to make a huge impact on the world. If Dragon takes action to realize dreams, there is no limit to the heights that can be achieved. If Dragon's idealism is not combined with concrete action, Dragon can turn into an indolent, discontented daydreamer who pays little attention to practicality and reality. Regardless of gender, Dragon tends to marry late in life, if at all, since he is unwilling to let go of dreams and adventures to live within the confines of an ordinary domestic life.

Dragon tends to not pay attention to details because he possesses a regal quality—someone else can take care of the petty stuff in life. Dragon believes that he is born for something on a grander scale. Many Dragons succeed in the world of entertainment.

One of Dragon's faults may be that he sometimes says or does things impulsively. This often causes social blunders. Another difficulty for Dragon is that life experiences are very intense because Dragon wears the horns of destiny. There are no casual friendships for Dragon. Every interaction is a continuation of heavy pastlife karma that must be resolved *now*. It is as if ten lifetimes are being lived out in the current incarnation.

DRAGON RELATIONSHIPS

Dragon with Rat: Mutual trust, understanding, and empathy make these two ideal lifelong partners. Dragons enjoy attention, and charming Rat is eager to appreciate, flatter, and praise mighty Dragon. Rat's thrifty ways and intelligent financial counsel help Dragon, who otherwise could squander large sums of money. Rat will be loyal to Dragon and blindly follow dynamic Dragon's lead. Sexually, this can be a most passionate and exciting combination.

Dragon with Ox: These two strong-willed personalities can clash. Both are used to having their own way and won't compromise. Quick, mercurial Dragon finds Ox a slow bore. Thorough, methodical Ox finds Dragon erratic and unpredictable. Practical Ox won't flatter Dragon because Ox isn't impressed by Dragon grandeur. Yet they respect each other in business.

Dragon with Tiger: Fearless Dragon and brave Tiger share a love of travel, progressive politics, and a thirst for excitement. Both value their freedom and independence, so neither one will be

dominated. They must work as a balanced team and not become competitors or rivals. Both start projects but don't finish them, so they may have a tendency to dream great schemes together but produce little.

Dragon with Hare: Dragon may be attracted to Hare's quiet charm and peaceful manners. Hare may be attracted to Dragon's charisma and power. Hare can help Dragon accomplish goals and further career ambitions. Hare knows how to compromise when Dragon won't. Dragon enjoys rescuing a Hare in distress and is strong in Hare's time of weakness. But Dragon may desire a more formidable partner, and finds shy Hare an uneven match, especially in temperament.

Dragon with Dragon: Two mighty Dragons together either move mountains and encourage each other to attain great heights or, together, they open the gates of hell as fierce rivals with each demanding total power. If they combine forces and learn to compromise, they can enjoy a rich life together. In a heterosexual relationship, a female Dragon is as strong as a male Dragon. The male Dragon must accept that a no-nonsense Dragon woman won't flatter and cajole her mate. In a homosexual relationship, this can be an especially dynamic partnership.

Dragon with Serpent: Together these two strong personalities can acquire much money and success. They both possess strong sexual appetites and find each other a dynamic lover. Dragon can help Serpent enjoy life. Serpent can help Dragon become more reflective. But Dragon is an extrovert and Serpent is an introvert. Dragon loves independence and freedom, and Serpent may try to control Dragon, resulting in Dragon feeling smothered and resentful.

Dragon with Horse: Although these two active and strong personalities may be physically compatible, they are emotionally incompatible. Dragon finds Horse selfish and egotistical, unwilling to offer Dragon the attention and support he desires. Dragon will not appreciate Horse's volatile temper. Independent Horse refuses to be dominated by Dragon and angrily resents Dragon's frank attempts to do so.

Dragon with Sheep: Dragon can enjoy a gentle and compassionate partner in Sheep. Both have much to gain in this relationship. Bighearted Dragon wants to help spiritual Sheep, who is kind to Dragon in return. These two lively types enjoy creative endeavors and a brisk social life. Sheep may have to toughen up to match Dragon. Regardless of gender, Dragon will dominate and initiate activities.

Dragon with Monkey: This partnership is one of the best combinations for Dragon because doubting Monkey trusts, respects, and appreciates magnificent Dragon. Monkey matches Dragon in power, intelligence, creativity, and entrepreneurial activity. Monkey's guile inspires Dragon to greater success, and helps Dragon develop confidence. They are both very strong, so their fights may be loud but brief.

Dragon with Phoenix: The union of these two mythical creatures is blessed by gods and goddesses in heaven. Between them there is a sense of a great love, a grand passion. Dragon and Phoenix make a striking couple, shine in the spotlight, and together can conquer the world. Dragon finds Phoenix's constant criticism and complaints to be amusing and witty. Dragon sees in Phoenix the potential for Phoenix to become truly transformed and overcome all obstacles with Dragon's love and support.

Dragon with Dog: Cynical Dog is not impressed by magnificent Dragon. Dragon enjoys flights of fantasy, and down-to-earth Dog refuses to be swept away. Dragon's dazzle may be ridiculed, his mighty fire extinguished, and all creative actions condemned. Avoid Dog, who is Dragon's opposite.

Dragon with Boar: Boar fawns over Dragon, who can benefit from this partnership. Sweet, kind Boar desires to take care of Dragon, allows Dragon his independence, and appreciates the lively good times that Dragon brings into Boar's life. Boar rarely fights, so Dragon can enjoy a smooth life when partnered with Boar. Finances should be watched, since both can be large spenders.

DRAGON CHILD AND PARENT

A Dragon child is born to lead and accomplish great things. Independent and able to take care of himself, he will not require constant supervision. A Dragon child is healthy, not needy, and obeys elders, parents, and teachers. He needs room to grow and explore, and a playground is Dragon child's perfect spot on earth. This child will not blossom if left in a small room to play quietly. Dragon is not home-oriented but expects adult caregivers to be reliable and to focus on the family. Because Dragon is greatly affected by past-life karma, childhood events and relations with parents and siblings are often intense. If sibling rivalry occurs, Dragon child must be kept in check and not be allowed to bully other children. If born during a storm, the child's path is extreme—either positive or negative. Being born during pouring rain augurs financial prosperity.

The Dragon parent is generous to his children, denying them nothing, and could spoil them. This outpouring of love and support masks a stern, authoritarian, and overprotective side. Firm Dragon can discipline strong-willed children, such as Tiger sons, Monkeys of both genders, and Horse daughters. The same rules of compatibility apply as for Dragon relationships: Dragon is most harmonious with Rat, Dragon, Monkey, and Phoenix children, who enjoy the fun outdoor activities the Dragon parent plans for them. Tiger, Hare, Serpent, and Sheep children can enjoy the security and amusement offered by a Dragon parent. Although Ox, Horse, and Dog children may feel misunderstood, the Dragon parent will strive to be fair with them.

DRAGON IN THE TWELVE-BRANCH CYCLE

Dragon in Rat year: This is one of the best years for Dragon because Rat is one of Dragon's closest friends. Rat's influence brings new beginnings and exciting creative endeavors that perfectly match Dragon's flamboyant style. Business interests prosper as does romance.

Dragon in Ox year: Expect a steady year of progress and the

reaping of activities begun in the previous Rat year. Problems
of those surrounding Dragon needn't effect him. But under Ox's
influence Dragon must work, not just dream.

Dragon in Tiger year: Tiger's influence brings much activity,
change, and volatile relationships. Fun, celebrations, and opportunities to shine will be balanced by worry, plans blocked
by others, and possibly stressful situations.

Dragon in Hare year: Expect peace, harmony, an opportunity to
retreat; a calm year of good fortune when home life is stable
and a favorable time to redecorate. Frivolous amusements will
be entertaining and enjoyable.

Dragon in Dragon year: Expect great accomplishments on a grand
scale, for Dragon benefits greatly from the energy of his own
year. Recognition is foreseen, much progress occurs in business, and exciting social activities create much happiness for
lucky Dragon.

Dragon in Serpent year: Good luck and positive acclaim continue, especially in business. But personal relationship problems concerning boundaries and responsibilities must be given
attention. Problematic romances must be healed or ended.

Dragon in Horse year: Expect some difficulties as Horse and
Dragon are not especially compatible. Dragon could feel insecure and nervous for unknown reasons, receive unpleasant news,
or have to change residence. Despite these difficulties, Dragon
emerges a leader.

Dragon in Sheep year: Expect social pleasantries and moderate
success in business. Affairs will run smoothly. It is best to remain aloof concerning others' incompetence and lack of desire
to work. Find time for vacation, ease, and comfort.

Dragon in Monkey year: Expect a wonderful year full of delightful surprises and opportunities for success because Monkey is
Dragon's best friend. Much progress is indicated, but avoid the
tendency to quarrel. Definitely avoid legal entanglements if
possible.

Dragon in Phoenix year: One of the best years of the twelve-
branch cycle because Dragon and Phoenix are harmonious.

Good fortune and prosperity continue from the previous Monkey year. Happiness, positive news, promotions, and business success are foreseen. New friends can offer positive opportunities and assistance.

Dragon in Dog year: Be ready for the most uncomfortable year of the twelve-branch cycle because Dog is Dragon's one enemy. Difficulties are foreseen, plans cannot manifest, and people seem contrary. Not a favorable year for marriage.

Dragon in Boar year: Life stabilizes after the challenges of the previous Dog year. Easy travel, light entertaining, and amusing recreation are enjoyable. Caution with finances is recommended since Dragon can overspend this year. Work tends to be mundane, slow, and perhaps a bit frustrating.

火龍 RED DRAGON—1916, 1976

Red Dragon is the fire Dragon. In its masculine, yang aspect, fire is symbolized by burning wood, the creative symbol of those born in the year of the red Dragon.

Red Dragon easily integrates fire characteristics—reason, expressiveness, spirituality, intuition, insight, dynamism, passion, aggressiveness, leadership, and gentility—into his extroverted personality because these qualities are natural Dragon traits (see page 18). The fire personality is direct and up-front. This perfectly suits red Dragon, who enjoys being the center of attention and has few problems with self-expression.

Red Dragon aspires to greatness and can change the world. The fiercest of all Dragons, he is extremely powerful and may be the strongest sign of the Taoist zodiac. Red Dragon is an aggressive leader who pursues goals and attains success by any means. Woe to anyone who crosses red Dragon, whose power can feel like a breath of fire that burns anyone who gets in the way.

Dragon's earthly branch is the element wood (see page 24). This alchemy is very favorable because wood feeds fire. Red Dragon is unstoppable in all efforts because his energy is constantly supplied by the wood earthly branch. Red Dragon possesses the abundant

energy necessary to pursue dreams and succeeds because of passion, power, and aggressiveness.

In relationships, red Dragon loves the chase and the beginning stages of courtship. After obtaining what he wants, he may
not stay with his partner. Fire can make for an erratic and unfaith-
ful partner. Unlike other Dragons who can be faithful, fidelity in
marriage is often a challenge for red Dragon.

When upset, red Dragon can become coldhearted, despotic,
irrational, critical, and unwilling to compromise. When balanced,
red Dragon has a sense of justice and knows when to stop. Red
Dragon succeeds by developing warmhearted generosity and
should seek joyful and pleasurable experiences.

土龍 YELLOW DRAGON—1928, 1988

Yellow Dragon is the earth Dragon. When embodying
masculine yang energy, earth's symbol is a hill. If you were
born in the year of the yellow Dragon, a hill or mountain is your
personal symbol.

Stability, honesty, practicality, industry, prudence, reliability,
kindness, and loyalty are earth qualities (see page 20). These characteristics enrich yellow Dragon's character and add much-needed
stability.

Dragon's earthly branch is the element wood (see page 24).
Earth nurtures wood, which slows down yellow Dragon. Therefore he is able to plan ahead, work hard, complete projects, and
view life realistically, unlike other Dragons who are impractical
and impulsively charge into any situation. A slower pace can help
yellow Dragon to evolve a spiritual side. When overwhelmed, yellow Dragon does well to meditate and contemplate. As he continues to grow spiritually, yellow Dragon can learn to appreciate the
beauty of a simple life.

Like all Dragons, yellow Dragon is regal and powerful and wants
to change the world. Yellow Dragon's magnanimous and liberal
attitude makes him a social activist who respects the rights of others. He is less dictatorial than other Dragons and can work collec-

tively. Still, as a Dragon he can be authoritarian at times. Yellow Dragon also excels in the business world where practical yet dynamic energy guarantees success.

Yellow Dragon is a cherished friend, a wonderful lover, and a trusted family member. Yellow Dragon easily demonstrates this sympathetic nature and shows much kindness to others. In partnerships, yellow Dragon is reliable, sincere, and faithful. He is very desirable as a marriage partner because he will stay committed after the initial pursue-and-conquer Dragon style of courtship. Yellow Dragon is intensely loyal and usually marries for life.

WHITE DRAGON—1940, 2000

White Dragon is the metal Dragon. When metal expresses masculine yang energy, it is symbolized by a weapon, the personal symbol of anyone born in this year.

Metal qualities are righteousness, independence, strong will, intensity, uprightness, determination, and ability to focus (see page 21). These qualities greatly empower white Dragon. White Dragon is known for excessive strength, daring, and courage. He is one of the most powerful signs of the Taoist zodiac.

White Dragon is an intense warrior who seeks action and adventure, like martial arts master Bruce Lee, the quintessential white Dragon. White Dragon wishes to be surrounded with only the finest companions and will not tolerate weakness and indecisiveness in others.

Few people possess white Dragon's ambition, creativity, fierce sexuality, and fanaticism. Born to achieve great success and transform the world, white Dragon cannot be bought or swayed once focused on a goal.

The earthly branch of Dragon is wood (see page 24). Wood has an antagonistic relationship to metal because metal cuts wood. This elemental alchemy can inhibit the emotional development of white Dragon. The metal nature can be cutting and result in a dual personality who experiences much inner conflict. In order to best integrate the metal and wood elements, white Dragon needs to become less intense, demanding, and stubborn. This is very challenging for the overly zealous, egocentric white Dragon. He is often self-righteous about trifles and can be extreme with criticisms and condemnations of others who are less obsessive and less driven.

In business, white Dragon is ruthless and competitive to a fault, destroying all enemies. In relationships, white Dragon can be tyrannical and insensitive to the emotions of a partner. He can create unbalanced relationships of codependence in which white Dragon is too controlling of his partner. White Dragon should strive to relinquish control and to not be stubborn and selfish. Fidelity is difficult for white Dragon, whose sex appeal and love of adventure cannot be stifled. He will be a loner rather than compromise.

Balanced metal makes white Dragon fair and patient. If metal qualities are undeveloped, he cannot make money or take care of themselves. This can be a Dragon problem, especially if white Dragon is a dreamer, not a doer, and has no outlet for his intense power.

To heal, white Dragon must learn to be tolerant and to gracefully release the past, including grief from previous relationships.

水 龍 BLACK DRAGON—1952, 2012

Black Dragon is the water Dragon. When water expresses masculine yang energy, it is symbolized by a wave. If you were born in the year of the black Dragon, your personal symbol is a cresting wave.

The most yin element, water softens Dragon in this combination (see page 22). Water qualities, including sensitivity, drive, effectiveness, creativity, and passion, enrich black Dragon and enable him to feel deeply and live life to the fullest.

Dragon's earthly branch is the element wood (see page 24). Water feeds wood and helps wood to grow. This helps black Dragon to easily nurture self and others with outstanding sensitivity and caring. Black Dragon is so nurturing to others because he knows how to care for himself.

Black Dragon is powerful, regal, strong, growth-oriented, sensual, and spiritual, a fervent believer in his chosen metaphysical path. Emotionally he is fiery and passionate, and often possesses a voracious sexual appetite. He has a reputation for being a great lover, sensual and passionate. Like all Dragons, he enjoys the chase of courtship. A mature black Dragon can be loyal in partnership.

In work, black Dragon is a confident self-starter who finishes projects. He is a perfectionist who can be very critical and impatient of self and others, possesses high standards, and won't settle for mediocrity. Black Dragon is less selfish and despotic than other Dragons, able to conform and devote himself for the common good. Kind by nature, he is rarely overtly cruel to others. Still, Dragon qualities can surface at times, and he can be self-centered. He doesn't care what "the little people" think and assumes that others are fortunate just to be in his presence. When overwhelmed, black Dragon can be frantic or overactive, especially if born during a storm. He should try to tackle fewer projects and not spread energies too thinly.

Black Dragon loves to travel the world and interact with a wide array of people. He must not allow fear to block the fullest expression of creativity. Black Dragon's challenge is to overcome fear and become an active participant in life.

木龍 GREEN DRAGON—1904, 1964

Green Dragon is the wood Dragon. When expressing masculine yang energy, wood is symbolized by a pine tree, sturdy and upright. If you were born in the year of the green Dragon, the pine is your totem.

Wood qualities are boldness, creativity, idealism, imagination, steadfastness, benevolence, competitiveness, and organization. These are natural Dragon characteristics (except organization), so green Dragon easily achieves goals.

The earthly branch of Dragon is of the element wood (see page 24). Therefore green Dragon has a double dose of wood's drive, growth, and enthusiasm. He idealistically embraces new projects, and is highly creative and dramatically imaginative.

Green Dragon is bold, dynamic, generous, talented, and intelligent. He is usually quite attractive physically and enjoys many admirers. Charismatic green Dragon is a sincere idealist who believes he can change the world. Revolutionary but not rebellious, green Dragon is inquisitive and always questions the societal norm. He follows the dictates of his own heart and can't be told by anyone what to do.

In work, green Dragon is competitive. He is an enthusiastic starter but one who often experiences difficulties completing projects and can be more of an inspired dreamer than a responsible doer. Green Dragon makes rash black-and-white decisions which are not always to his advantage. He wants events to proceed as he dictates, and will leave abruptly if he cannot have his way. Green Dragon's career is often chaotic in early life. He is a late bloomer who steadily grows into formidable power.

When challenged, green Dragon can be stubborn and prejudiced. Undeveloped wood can make green Dragon an unreliable person who lacks direction. This can be a problem during youth, especially if green Dragon is a dreamer.

Balanced wood can make green Dragon flexible and openminded. Green Dragon's challenge is to control anger and channel it into positive, socially beneficial actions.

SERPENT

Keywords: Wisdom, mystery, sensuality.
Serpent correlates to the Western sign Taurus.

SERPENT LUNAR CALENDAR

1905—February 4 to January 24, 1906	Blue Serpent
1917—January 23 to February 10, 1918	Purple Serpent
1929—February 10 to January 29, 1930	Gold Serpent
1941—January 27 to February 14, 1942	Silver Serpent
1953—February 14 to February 2, 1954	Gray Serpent
1965—February 2 to January 20, 1966	Blue Serpent
1977—February 18 to February 6, 1978	Purple Serpent
1989—February 16 to January 26, 1990	Gold Serpent
2001—January 24 to February 11, 2002	Silver Serpent
2013—February 10 to January 30, 2014	Gray Serpent
2025—January 29 to February 16, 2026	Blue Serpent

SERPENT YEAR

The Chinese Serpent goddess Nu Kua formed the first people from yellow clay from the banks of the Yellow River. This creation myth is one of many Taoist tales starring magical, mysterious Serpent. The Serpent is associated with goddesses and heroines who assist women in childbirth and bless children with remarkable talents. Serpent heroines charmed and helped scholars learn the Confucian classics. Asian cultures respect Serpent and honor her feminine yin energy, unlike the West, which associates Serpent with cold-blooded evils.

The Chinese classic tale tells of a one-thousand-year-old serpent who practiced magic and transformed herself into a beautiful woman. Through her charms, she married a scholar, and her life was happy and content. But a Taoist monk pursued her because he knew that she was not human. The monk was an expert at capturing shape-shifting animals who falsely assumed human forms. Wise Serpent outwitted him many times before he finally exposed her dual lives.

The year of the Serpent is a time of introspection, planning, and seeking answers. People will ponder and think before they act. Good taste and elegance will prevail in fashion, theater, film, and all the arts. Serpent wisdom influences contributions in the sciences through new technological inventions and discoveries. But this is not an auspicious year for gambling, investing, or taking any financial risks because the calamities of the previous Dragon year can continue into Serpent year. Expect political extremes, scandals, and the exposing of secrets.

SERPENT PERSONALITY

Enchanting Serpent is creative, attractive, and talented. The Serpent individual is very sociable and loves making friends and creating contacts and networks. But she can appear cool and aloof at times. Serpent possesses both charm and a mysterious quality, yet she won't easily reveal her thoughts to anyone. If she allows you to get close, you will discover that Serpent is a sensitive, caring, compassionate, and humorous person.

Serpent is extremely determined and strives for things she desires regardless of circumstances. Unlike Dragon who accomplishes set goals through intense outward actions and activities, Serpent accomplishes her goals through careful plans and calculations. Serpent is not afraid to take risks and has immense mental capacity to turn the outcome in her favor.

A great observer of human nature, Serpent has keen perceptions. Rarely is she openly aggressive, even though she may be secretly plotting the next move. Serpent has incredible patience to wait silently until the time is right. When attacking a target, she is swift and focused and rarely misses.

In ancient Taoism, Serpent is the symbol of wisdom. One born in a Serpent year is usually philosophical and spiritual, with wisdom and grace. But Serpent must not let her contemplative nature become overly pensive, brooding, or moody.

Serpent possesses especially fine taste in fashion and her clothing reflects artistry and creativity. Serpent can be frugal if necessary, although she prefers the luxury of a materially rich life.

Both romantic relationships and family are important parts of Serpent's life, so she usually marries early. Female or male, Serpents are generally very attractive and their mystical and mysterious personalities only add to their charm. Rarely are they concerned with a lack of suitors.

A natural philosopher and theologian who likes to coil up and contemplate, Serpent is psychologically complex. Just as Dragon's external events tend to be grand, Serpent's inner life is especially rich and detailed. Serpent constantly analyzes, scrutinizes, probes, and questions.

On the negative side, Serpent needs to curb her immense pride and the tendency to want things her way. This could make Serpent uncompromising and jealous in relationships. Serpent can be ruthless when challenged. Since she is the master of the human psyche, this makes Serpent a formidable enemy.

SERPENT RELATIONSHIPS

Serpent with Rat: Amorous Serpent can be sexually compatible with romantic Rat, who offers Serpent the love and devotion she craves. Together they can make a financial fortune because ambitious, clever Rat can inspire strong, cunning Serpent to succeed. But Serpent must not be too possessive with Rat, who is a natural flirt.

Serpent with Ox: Together they share quiet sympathy and mutual

understanding. Wise Serpent likes to ponder and discuss while Ox enjoys listening and learning. Serpent appreciates her captive audience and Ox is charmed by Serpent's positive qualities. Insecure Serpent can rely on faithful Ox to be supportive and responsible. Both share similar values and together make excellent parents. This deep relationship can last a lifetime.

Serpent with Tiger: Serpent may be attracted to Tiger's physicality and Tiger may be attracted to Serpent's elusive charm and beauty. (Tiger enjoys a hunt.) But Serpent is basically incompatible with Tiger. Serpent likes to ponder and question while Tiger likes to jump impulsively and ponder later, if at all. Tiger's enthusiasm can overwhelm Serpent's genteel sensibilities. Conflict occurs when Serpent's needs are too demanding and possessive for freedom-loving Tiger.

Serpent with Hare: These two lovers of beauty share artistic interests and an exalted sense of aesthetics. Serpent is naturally comfortable with gentle Hare who, like Serpent, is intelligent, elegant, cultivated, and refined. Together they can create a beautiful home environment. Unless Hare was born during the hours of a strong animal, Serpent may find Hare too weak and indecisive to become a serious partner.

Serpent with Dragon: Dragon is one of the best partners for Serpent. Serpent finds Dragon's life to be fun, complex, and filled with fascinating intrigues, making Serpent stimulated and interested. Together these two formidable personalities can acquire much money and success. Both of these powerful signs possess strong sexual appetites and find each other a dynamic lover. But Serpent must allow Dragon her freedom.

Serpent with Serpent: Two Serpents can be a harmonious pair because they are both philosophers and artists, but they can become jealous and untrusting of each other. Over time, expect power struggles between these two strong and passionate personalities. If Serpents come to an understanding and do not allow mutual jealousy and suspicion to destroy their bond, they can enjoy their relationship.

Serpent with Horse: These are two very different personality types. Serpent is an introverted intellectual while Horse is an extroverted adventurer. Serpent plans for the future, while Horse lives in the moment. In a relationship, Serpent finds Horse irresponsible, inconsistent, and too selfish to dedicate herself exclusively to lovely Serpent. Serpent is possessive of wild Horse, who has difficulties with fidelity.

Serpent with Sheep: Penetrating Serpent and generous Sheep have little in common, except for their love of the arts. Determined Serpent aggressively pursues goals, while peaceful Sheep would rather change course when faced with challenges. Disciplined Serpent will not respect Sheep's artistic whims and may find Sheep sentimental and clinging. Sheep finds Serpent too complicated, demanding, and difficult to continue their relationship.

Serpent with Monkey: Serpent finds a strong and worthy partner in intelligent Monkey, who inspires Serpent to perform her best. Together they share stimulating conversation and similar values. This pair can acquire wealth and achieve success and status.

Serpent with Phoenix: Phoenix is an outstanding partner for Serpent. Both are intelligent, creative, interested in financial success, and know the value of hard work. But Serpent must accept Phoenix's fussiness and complaining. In return, Phoenix can appreciate Serpent's flexibility and willingness to listen and solve problems. They have potential for a solid relationship that reaps many rewards over time.

Serpent with Dog: Although Serpent and Dog can enjoy each other's company, calculating Serpent has very different values than fair-minded Dog. Serpent desires wealth and power while Dog desires truth and righteous action. Serpent may find Dog too simple and one-dimensional to hold her interest. Dog may find Serpent vain and impractical. In a relationship, Dog will resist possessive Serpent's attempts to curtail her freedom.

Serpent with Boar: Determined Serpent's values differ from those of carefree, affable Boar. Serpent's depth of mind is not interesting to Boar, who has no desire to contemplate mysteries. Boar's naiveté and innocence antagonize Serpent, who would never be so trusting. In frustration, Serpent may attempt to transform Boar into a sophisticate. This will be impossible, and Boar will resent being a plaything.

SERPENT CHILD AND PARENT

The Serpent child will succeed in life through sheer willpower and desire. She is extremely intelligent, so enrolling your Serpent child in advanced specialized schools is recommended. An outstanding scholar, the Serpent child enjoys her studies and strives to be teacher's pet.

Expect a Serpent child to be moody, a worrier, secretive, and temperamental. These emotional spells must be curbed, not indulged, by parents. The Serpent child is generally popular, yet will cultivate only one or two intimate friendships. The Serpent born during hot summer months is more venomous and driven to succeed. The winter-born Serpent is a quieter and calmer child, for that is the season when Serpents hibernate.

The Serpent parent is reliable and conscientious. Her innate Serpent wisdom can answer children's endless questions and calm their fears. But the Serpent parent insists on knowing her children's secrets and won't allow privacy, which may encourage children to lie.

The same rules of compatibility apply as for Serpent relationships: Serpent is most comfortable with Ox, Phoenix, and Dragon children who appreciate the security and constancy that Serpent parent provides. Rat, Hare, Serpent, and Sheep children enjoy the lovely surroundings of a Serpent home. Serpent may have problems with Tiger, Horse, Monkey, Dog, and Boar children. Tiger, Horse, and Monkey are very independent and resist being smothered by Serpent parent. Dog and Boar children will become upset when Serpent parent bends the truth or invades their privacy.

SERPENT IN THE TWELVE-BRANCH CYCLE

Serpent in Rat year: Expect hectic activity, which may overwhelm Serpent with responsibilities. If Serpent remains calm and centered and addresses each problem as it arises, progress can be attained, especially in business. It is best to be frugal and not spend or loan at this time.

Serpent in Ox year: This is a fortunate time because Ox is Serpent's good friend, but Serpent will be asked to work. Unlike the previous Rat year, Serpent's toiling will be rewarded. But do not allow Ox's stubborn influence to make Serpent unreasonable or demanding. Intelligent compromise benefits everyone.

Serpent in Tiger year: Difficulties and calamities result from the activities of others. Too many circumstances are not in Serpent's control, which Serpent does not like. Coarse Tiger energy is antithetical to Serpent's refined sensibilities.

Serpent in Hare year: Enjoy the arts, indulge in fine fashions and cuisine, and relax during pleasant holidays. Success is foreseen, although these good times can be expensive.

Serpent in Dragon year: Expect excitement and much activity. It is best if Serpent retreats occasionally from all the action to quietly ponder and meditate. In this way, Serpent retains power in the eye of the storm and ends the year with a full harvest.

Serpent in Serpent year: Good fortune reigns as Serpent benefits from the influence of her own year. Much is accomplished without risk, finances are bountiful, and relationships are harmonious.

Serpent in Horse year: Expect a Horse year to bring calamity, such as emotional problems, misunderstandings, and miscommunications. Relationships, particularly romantic ones, can suffer. Serpent benefits by protecting her health and avoiding emotional extremes.

Serpent in Sheep year: Expect lovely social times, which can become dramatic if taken to extremes. Not much will be accomplished, although Serpent enjoys pretty artifice. Charming new friends will prove valuable in later years.

Serpent in Monkey year: Expect wild turmoil and extremes under Monkey's influence. Serpent can survive and become a winner if she remains neutral and relies on innate Serpent wisdom and intuition as guidance.

Serpent in Phoenix year: Superb fortune is probable because Phoenix is one of the best companions for Serpent. Recognition, rewards, promotions, and bonuses are foreseen. Serpent is feted and enjoys popularity, but Serpent must contribute at work and save money.

Serpent in Dog year: Expect problems concerning values, viewpoints, and ideologies. But if Serpent keeps opinions and insights private, much can be accomplished. A time for new endeavors as opportunities for advancement arise.

Serpent in Boar year: Accomplishments will be negligible as Serpent completes the twelve-branch cycle. Plans may not manifest, and it is best to look forward to auspicious new beginnings in the next Rat year. Even though Boar is Serpent's opposite and foe, perhaps Serpent can enjoy the leisure and indulgence that a Boar year brings.

火 蛇 PURPLE SERPENT—1917, 1977

Purple Serpent is the fire Serpent. When it embodies feminine yin energy, fire is symbolized by the flame of a lamp. If you were born in the year of the purple Serpent, a pure flame is your personal symbol for meditation.

Fire qualities—reason, expressiveness, spirituality, intuition, insight, dynamism, passion, aggressiveness, leadership, and good manners—give purple Serpent a lively personality. Unlike other Serpents, purple Serpent is an extrovert. Unlike other Serpents, purple Serpent often says what she thinks and does what she wants without much thought to the consequences.

The earthly branch of Serpent is the element fire (see page 18). Purple Serpent, with a double dose of fire's passion, intensity, and spirituality, is extremely charismatic, powerful, and attractive. She makes a good, firm leader and refuses to follow or bow down to others.

Purple Serpent will succeed in endeavors because she is a dynamic worker and will do almost anything to attain prosperity. She sets goals and swiftly accomplishes tasks. No project is too intimidating for this powerful, results-oriented personality. She makes fast decisions by seeing situations in black or white. If taken to extreme, purple Serpent can become selfish, egocentric, and power hungry. A purple Serpent born in the hot months of summer can become ruthless and aggressive when competing with rivals.

Purple Serpent lives life on a grand scale. She craves material comfort and fine surroundings. Purple Serpent desires to be the center of attention and may dress flamboyantly. She loves to entertain and enjoys a large circle of friends and confidants. She enjoys all the arts, especially dance and theater. At times, purple Serpent may have to temper some of her fiery personality traits to be more compatible with gentler people.

Purple Serpent finds happiness through warmhearted generosity. The Serpent's suspicious nature must be transformed to the realization that the world is not out to get the Serpent. Lack of trust must be replaced with acceptance and forgiveness.

土蛇 GOLD SERPENT—1929, 1989

Gold Serpent is the earth Serpent. When earth expresses feminine yin energy, it is represented by a valley. A lush valley is where you will be most content if you were born in the year of the gold Serpent.

Those born in a gold year are guarded, safe, protected and blessed by good fortune. This comfortable Serpent will always find the necessities of food and shelter—even strangers will help her.

Earth qualities are stability, honesty, practicality, industry, prudence, reliability, kindness, and loyalty (see page 20). Earth qualities add range to gold Serpent's character and make her less self-centered than other Serpents.

Serpent's earthly branch is the element fire (see page 18). Fire nurtures earth because after fire burns ash is created, which makes more earth. Therefore gold Serpent is very blessed. She embodies the finest qualities of the Serpent coupled with the good fortune of the golden one. She can realistically accomplish tasks and find peace and happiness. Gold Serpent succeeds by demonstrating her sympathetic nature and showing great kindness to others.

Gold Serpent's warm personality is appreciated by many, and her innate Serpent charm and elegance wins many admirers. Well loved and appreciated by friends and family members, gold Serpent is less ruthless when achieving goals than other Serpents. This wise soul values love more than money and harmony more than competition.

Gold Serpent does not have to work hard in life because acquiring material goods is not her prime ambition. Gold Serpent knows how to trust, unlike other Serpents who are always suspicious of the motives of others. When she does work, she exhibits high principles and integrity. Finances are rarely a problem for gold Serpent. She can invest well and succeed in real estate and the business world. She could be content in the arts as a designer or decorator.

Gold Serpent is strong and decisive. She communicates well and is steady in times of trouble due to her cool head, reserved nature, and powerful Serpent presence. She is reliable and loyal due to the earth influence. At times gold Serpent may be slow to react, but her conclusions are correct.

金 蛇 SILVER SERPENT—1941, 2001

Silver Serpent is the metal Serpent. When metal expresses feminine yin energy, it is symbolized by a kettle or cauldron, the emblem of the silver Serpent.

Metal qualities, including righteousness, independence, strong will, intensity, uprightness, determination, and ability to focus, add much power to silver Serpent (see page 21). Silver Serpent's dynamic willpower, ruthless ambition, and impeccable style guarantee that she will achieve a successful position in life. Metal is a symbol of wealth, and silver Serpent wants all the luxuries that wealth can purchase. She craves only the finest things in life. Silver Serpent's megalomaniacal quests for material gain and status result in secretive and often unscrupulous tactics. She will overcome obstacles to acquire money and success and do anything in her formidable power to win, and win she shall.

Silver Serpent is born to lead and command, and can destroy those who try to oppose her. She excels in the business world because she is ahead of the competition. Her brilliant and intelligent mind seizes every opportunity for advancement. Silver Serpent swiftly attacks the target before opponents realize what happened. The silver Serpent born in the hot summer months can exhibit excessively competitive behavior with rivals. Rarely satisfied, she is envious of the success of others. Suspicious Serpent trusts no one, so she is often a loner.

In speech, silver Serpent can be excessively aggressive and argumentative and may threaten the milder signs of the Taoist zodiac. In relationships, silver Serpent can create difficult partnerships, tending to overpower and squeeze partners like a boa constrictor. Silver Serpent's strong will and focused determination can manifest as overly dominant behavior. Silver Serpent does well to allow partners some independence and to be more sensitive and tolerant. When she cannot have her own way, silver Serpent must refrain from indulging in the dramatic role of emotional victim.

Serpent's earthly branch is the element fire (see page 18). Fire has an antagonistic relationship with metal because fire melts metal.

Silver Serpent can shed her skin and create true transformation by embracing the passion and love of the fire element. In this way, all the power and magnificence of silver Serpent can be transmuted to work toward a higher goal that includes all of humanity, instead of a selfish path that leads to alienation. (Pablo Picasso is an example of a transformed silver Serpent.)

Silver Serpent is generous to those she deems worthy and when reciprocity is guaranteed. Silver Serpent's challenge is to learn how to accept change, express emotions, including grief, and to release the constant desire to control situations.

水 蛇 GRAY SERPENT—1953, 2013

Gray Serpent is the water Serpent. When water expresses feminine yin energy, it is symbolized by a brook. If you were born in the year of the gray Serpent, your personal symbol is a clear brook.

Softened by the water qualities of sensitivity, drive, effectiveness, creativity, and passion, gray Serpent values family and friends. Serpent traits are especially in agreement with the water qualities of sensitivity, creativity, and the potential to attract (see page 22).

Charismatic gray Serpent is astute, highly intelligent, and possesses a good memory and a fine mind for details. She is quick to understand abstract concepts and can plan wisely. Her advanced intellect and unique creativity help her to guarantee success.

Like all Serpents, gray Serpent desires money, power, and prestige. Gray Serpent particularly craves excessive wealth and guaranteed financial security. She is intense and driven when pursuing goals, especially in the pursuit of riches. She wants to control her environment and the people in it.

Talented in handling and investing money, gray Serpent is shrewd, clever, and very materialistic in business transactions. In competition, gray Serpent can become tense or frantic unless she was born in winter when Serpent hibernates.

Serpent's earthly branch is the element fire (see page 18). Water extinguishes fire, so gray Serpent's personality exhibits fewer overtly fiery, combative, venomous, and critical characteristics than other Serpents. Instead, gray Serpent is more empathetic, emotional, and appreciative of beauty, peace, fashion, and the arts.

Because water extinguishes fire, gray Serpent may be thwarted and frustrated when trying to achieve goals. This will force gray Serpent to work harder to attain prosperity. Gray Serpent may experience moments of disappointment while fighting for success. After rest and retreat, gray Serpent will be able to forge ahead and learn from her setbacks. Water adds the power to swim through any crisis.

木 BLUE SERPENT—1905, 1965

虫它 Blue Serpent is the wood Serpent. The flexible bamboo that bends gently with the winds symbolizes the feminine yin energy aspects of wood. Bamboo is the tree totem of those born in the year of the blue Serpent.

Wood qualities include boldness, creativity, idealism, imagination, planning, steadfastness, benevolence, and competitiveness (see page 24). These characteristics add much drive and focus to blue Serpent, who is adept at initiating and achieving her goals.

Blue Serpent possesses the classic Serpent wisdom and intellect. The element wood pushes blue Serpent's philosophical mind to create a personal myth from the historical events of the past. She is a spiritual seeker who adores theater, painting, film, and all the decorative arts.

Like all Serpents, blue Serpent desires prosperity, status, and security. She succeeds due to a creative mind and good head for business. Blue Serpent writes and speaks well and is especially talented in the art of communication. Her risk-taking abilities and bravery help to outdistance rivals and win in most situations. She has the potential to accomplish outstanding achievements.

Blue Serpent desires only the finest things that money can buy and is most comfortable wearing well-made clothing. Materialistic competition can cause her to become vain and snobbish. Blue Serpent feels justified in this arrogance because she possesses a fine critical eye and encyclopedic knowledge.

Serpent's earthly branch is the element fire (see page 18). Wood helps fire to grow and burn brighter. Blue Serpent's energy shines brightly and powerfully, attracting people from all walks of life. At times blue Serpent may have to sacrifice for others, which she usually resents. It is helpful for blue Serpent to remain flexible when required to assist others and to channel her anger into positive achievements.

HORSE

Key words: Good humor, friendli-
ness, carefree attitude.
Horse correlates to the Western
sign Gemini.

HORSE LUNAR CALENDAR

1906—January 25 to February 12, 1907   Red Horse
1918—February 11 to January 31, 1919   Yellow Horse
1930—January 30 to February 16, 1931   White Horse
1942—February 15 to February 4, 1943   Black Horse
1954—February 3 to January 23, 1955   Green Horse
1966—January 21 to February 8, 1967   Red Horse
1978—February 7 to January 27, 1979   Yellow Horse
1990—January 27 to February 14, 1991   White Horse
2002—February 12 to January 31, 2003   Black Horse
2014—January 31 to February 18, 2015   Green Horse
2026—February 17 to February 5, 2027   Red Horse

HORSE YEAR

Powerful Horse has magical qualities, including the ability to fly.
A white (metal) celestial cloud horse was sacred to the compassionate goddess Kwan Yin (known as Kwannon in Japan). Kwan
Yin's white horse flies through the heavens, bringing peace and
blessings. The horse is descended from a region in upper Asia, and
the ancestor of all horses was the strong celestial charger of the

horse king, Ma-wang. Horse breeding was a highly developed art and the hobby of emperors in classical China, especially during the T'ang dynasty (A.D. 618 to 905). Great dynasties expanded and wars were won thanks to the horse, which is revered in China.

The year of the Horse is a time of victory, adventure, exciting activities, and surprising romances. Decisive action, not procrastination, brings success. Energy is high and production is rewarded. A Horse year marks the middle of the twelve-branch cycle and is the culmination of activities begun six years ago. Actions and achievements during this important year can influence the direction of the remaining years of the twelve-branch cycle. On a global scale, expect world economies to become stronger and industrial manufacturing to rise—or expect economic chaos and collapse, such as World War One in 1918, a yellow Horse year, or the Great Depression in the 1930s, which began in a white Horse year. Under strong Horse's influence, there is no middle ground.

Horse Personality

Horse is bright, open, cheerful, popular, and fun loving. Possessing a sunny disposition and natural charm, Horse finds people and crowds exciting and loves parties. His childlike innocence often attracts many friends, and he is not a loner. Horse is stimulated by film, theater, and most forms of entertainment.

Horse pays great attention to appearance and prefers fine clothing. Often Horse tends to be extravagant and will spend money needlessly in order to impress companions. When he likes something, he will usually purchase it regardless of cost.

Horse is frank and dislikes hidden agendas. He will tell you what is on his mind. Horse dislikes wishy-washy people and prefers to resolve problems in a quick and direct manner. At times Horse's quick opinions may alienate friends.

In general, Horse can enjoy a carefree life. Usually he doesn't need to struggle in order to succeed and obtain the fine things life has to offer. Because Horse is an intuitive animal, the Horse individual follows hunches. Characteristic keen judgment and natural intuition often help him make the right decisions throughout life.

In romance and relationships, Horse is idealistic and devoted. He prefers a lively partner who enjoys dancing, parties, travel, and various social activities. Yet Horse can become jealous and suspecting because of his competitive nature.

Horse participates in activities he enjoys, such as team sports, with the energy of a wild horse. Like running in a championship race, Horse often excels with unparalleled passion once his mind is set to accomplish something. Yet sometimes he changes his mind before completing a project, giving others the impression of irresponsibility. This behavioral pattern of stopping before completion may result from being born halfway through the twelve-branch cycle.

Rebelliousness is a difficult Horse trait. Because of his carefree nature, Horse needs ample room for self-expression. When put into a constrained environment and restricted by rules, he can become bitter and exhibit destructive behavior. Proud Horse refuses to be corralled or tamed. Also, Horse can become overtly jealous and offensive if he senses that someone else is valued more or treated better. Horse reacts by competing and promoting himself in order to win favor.

HORSE RELATIONSHIPS

Horse with Rat: Rat may be the worst mate for Horse. Honest Horse is an open, direct soul who dislikes hidden agendas or half-truths. Rat is born with hidden agendas, crafty secrets, and invents his own version of the truth. Horse enjoys unscheduled freedom, is popular with everyone, and is a big spender. Rat prefers meticulous planning, is charming only to those deemed worthy, and hoards money. Rat and Horse have very different values and little in common. Avoid Rat, who is Horse's opposite.

Horse with Ox: Horse may feel restrained by practical Ox, who criticizes Horse's laziness and is not enticed by Horse's exciting lifestyle. Ox works hard and expects his partner to share the weight of the yoke. Horse has no desire to become a

harnessed team animal, hauling the weight of the world. Horse is a free gypsy, whereas Ox values security and family. Horse may find Ox slow, boring, and too serious. They cannot have fun together, and Horse loves fun.

Horse with Tiger: Strong Tiger may be the best mate for Horse. They are sexually and emotionally compatible. Both Horse and Tiger share a love of fun, excitement, celebrations, travel, and impulsive wild adventures. Since they desire freedom, neither will be clingy or demanding of the other. Together they enjoy direct, frank communications. In Tiger's company, Horse can blossom and his best qualities have opportunities to develop. Over time, they can sustain their initial sexual attraction.

Horse with Hare: A friendship may be possible, but a deeper relationship with Hare may be difficult for Horse to sustain. Horse's direct style of communication and powerful physical presence may overwhelm diplomatic Hare, who prefers a genteel, refined mate. Horse may have to adjust his extreme temperament to match Hare's quiet nature. This puts a strain on Horse, who does not want to edit his words and suppress his actions. Horse may find Hare too weak and unable to keep up with Horse's active and varied lifestyle.

Horse with Dragon: Horse may enjoy Dragon's company, but

Dragon may not always enjoy Horse's company. Dragon could secretly resent Horse if he does not offer Dragon total dedication. Instead, Horse prefers to place Horse first. Both Horse and Dragon are aggressive, but have different goals, so a personality clash can occur. If a power struggle results, Dragon will insist on winning, whereas Horse would rather quit and move on to the next adventure.

Horse with Serpent: These two are usually incompatible in any kind of partnership. Horse is direct and Serpent is complex. Horse loves crowds, excitement, and interacting with all types of people; Serpent is basically an introvert who would rather contemplate and read philosophy. Serpent plans for the future, while passionate Horse lives for the moment. Serpent may try to prevent Horse from galloping off on his next wild adventure by slowly coiling around the object of his affections. Horse must escape or be smothered.

Horse with Horse: Two Horses make a good team, not competitive rivals, and can experience many exciting adventures together. They have similar values and personality traits. Both know how to enjoy life and take it easy, not worry and fuss. Horses are great conversationalists and can discuss events together for hours. Both have short fuses, but they quickly forget after a temperamental blowup occurs. Horse understands and forgives the other's lack of firm commitments, big ego, and unreliability. Finances must be watched or serious debt may result.

Horse with Sheep: Horse can find lasting happiness, emotional support, and inspiration from beautiful, artistic Sheep. Kind Sheep encourages Horse's finest performance and forgives Horse any of his selfish shortcomings. Social Sheep enjoys Horse's wild adventures and appreciates new experiences. Sheep's usual clinging behavior will be interpreted as devotion and dedication by Horse. Gentle Sheep knows best how to handle Horse's volatile temper and calm him down. Regardless of gender, Horse's dominant personality will direct this relationship.

Horse with Monkey: These two dominant and powerful personalities share many admirable qualities. Both are aggressive,

strong-minded, outgoing, fun-loving, entertaining, enthusiastic, and colorful. But honest Horse may not trust trickster
Monkey. Both are lively talkers, but in conversation direct
Horse distrusts Monkey's evasive tactics. Horse's intuitive sense
detects secretive Monkey's hidden agendas and that Monkey
does not tell all he knows. Scrupulous Horse may find Monkey an opportunist, causing Horse to be on guard.

Horse with Phoenix: Superficially, Horse and Phoenix enjoy social affairs, are frank and direct talkers, and make an attractive
pair. But this is basically an antagonistic relationship. Phoenix
cannot refrain from criticizing Horse, a free spirit with a gypsy
heart. Phoenix may accuse Horse of being a lazy, disorganized
dreamer who lacks foresight and dedication to Phoenix's materialistic goals.

Horse with Dog: This is one of the best relationships for Horse
in the entire twelve-branch cycle. Honest, frank Horse seeks a
partner who possesses integrity, loyalty, intelligence, and dedication to altruistic goals. Dog is perfectly suited to fulfill Horse's
ideals. Dog understands Horse very well, is not offended by
Horse's direct statements or sudden changes in plans, and is
one of the few who can calm Horse's temper. Horse finds it
easy to be faithful to his trusty Dog. This relationship can last
a lifetime.

Horse with Boar: These two sensual and indulgent personalities
enjoy the fine things in life, but their temperaments differ. Horse
is much stronger and bolder than obliging Boar, who dislikes
fighting and becomes uneasy when Horse's temper flares. Even
if Boar is unhappy, Boar fears change and may manipulate Horse
in order to make their relationship last. Horse unwittingly may
be too selfish or self-centered for the generous Boar, who sacrifices too much and plays the role of martyr.

HORSE CHILD AND PARENT

The Horse child is lively, independent, talkative, and mercurial.
He loves the outdoors, and the playground and beach are favorite

places. Horse matures quickly and possesses the ability to do many different projects at once. Parents and teachers may be amazed by his rapid development. But it may be difficult for a parent or teacher who attempts to restrain little Horse. Expect a strong, willful child who resists authority. A Horse child must be taught to share and to control his temper.

Horse has a better life if born in the winter. Otherwise he may become overworked, toiling in the fields in spring, summer, and fall. Work is not Horse's strong point.

The Horse parent may have other priorities than just child rearing, including a career. Horses are not particularly home oriented and tend to neglect some parental duties. The same rules of compatibility apply as for Horse relationships: Horse is most harmonious with Tiger, Horse, Sheep, and Dog children, who can play independently and don't need, or want, a parent to discipline them. Dragon, Monkey, Phoenix, and Boar children make the best of the situation and don't demand much from the Horse parent. Horse may have problems with Rat, Ox, and Serpent children, who require security, routine, and more attention than the Horse parent has time to give.

HORSE IN THE TWELVE-BRANCH CYCLE

Horse in Rat year: Expect difficulties because Rat is opposite Horse in the twelve-branch cycle. Conflict can occur in romance, in business, and with authority figures including the law. Horse benefits from prudent spending, disciplined work, and behaving less free spirited.

Horse in Ox year: Expect easier and smoother circumstances than in the previous Rat year. Horse can succeed by maintaining more control in personal interactions, although romantic relationships may be problematic. Ox's influence demands work, which is not Horse's favorite activity.

Horse in Tiger year: Happy times predominate because Tiger is Horse's best friend. Entertainment may be expensive, but this year is the time for Horse to live well. Horse regains popularity and enjoys robust health. But he must not lose his temper or succumb to impulsive outbursts.

Horse in Hare year: Expect good fortune and lucky circumstances—romance, social activities, and business can flourish. It is an especially good time for investments, marriage, politics, and adding new family members.

Horse in Dragon year: Expect extremes of highs and lows under Dragon's stormy influence. Horse may feel unsettled and start to worry, which is not a common Horse response. Horse benefits by enjoying the company of family and friends and by not cultivating a fearful or pessimistic attitude.

Horse in Serpent year: This busy year involves some difficulties from partners, delays in business, and general frustrations. If a new romance develops, it is likely to be short-lived. Perhaps Horse can find solace from close friends and family, as in the previous Dragon year.

Horse in Horse year: Expect a good and prosperous year because Horse benefits from the influence of his own year. Horse can achieve recognition and satisfaction in work, plans can be realized with ease, and lucky new endeavors result from following his intuition.

Horse in Sheep year: Expect a calm and easy year because Horse and Sheep are friends. Horse has opportunities to complete endeavors begun in the previous Horse year. Improved health, a long vacation, and good news are foreseen.

Horse in Monkey year: Monkey's crazy influence brings wild luck and sudden gains. Horse can find what he seeks, play politics, and have fun. But be cautious to avoid accidents, especially when driving or using metal tools for cutting.

Horse in Phoenix year: Expect a harmonious year that brings good news. Home life is stable and problems are not overwhelming. But Horse may be required to work harder and slow down his development, which Horse will not like.

Horse in Dog year: Expect an exemplary year because Horse and Dog are great friends. Horse can succeed in business and academics and accomplish his goals. Important and influential people guide him and offer opportunities for advancement.

Horse in Boar year: This year brings some unfavorable circumstances. Difficulties with coworkers and miscommunications can delay success. Horse may overspend on luxuries, such as a new car. Life becomes less stressful at the onset of winter.

火馬 RED HORSE—1906, 1966, 2026

Red Horse is the infamous fire Horse. When fire expresses masculine yang energy, it is symbolized by burning wood, the creative symbol of those born in the year of the red Horse.

Fire qualities are reason, expressiveness, spirituality, intuition, insight, dynamism, passion, aggressiveness, leadership, and gentility. All Horses naturally possess some fiery attributes, especially directness, intuition, dynamism, and passion. Red Horse benefits from fire's qualities, especially reason and a proper sense of etiquette.

Fire is Horse's earthly branch (see page 18). With a double dose of fire's vitality, red Horse's magnetic personality and sex appeal are enticing to many. He is strong, passionate, and single-minded—no one can tell a red Horse what to do.

Horses are known as work animals, but red Horse refuses to work hard. Red Horse is brilliantly talented in many areas, but at the same time can be easily distracted and bored. Instead of applying himself to a task, he is off to discover the latest distraction. Red Horse often does not complete projects. If disciplined, however, success can be achieved. Red Horse's strong willpower can transform a difficult circumstance into a winning situation. He is not afraid to confront difficult issues, and desires immediate resolution of conflicts.

Like all fire signs, red Horse enjoys travel and adventure, finding remote uncharted areas of the world most interesting. Red Horse possesses an uncanny intuition, enabling him to recognize an opportunity and to avoid danger.

Balanced fire creates a Horse with a sense of justice who knows when to stop. Red Horse succeeds by developing warmhearted generosity.

土 馬 YELLOW HORSE—1918, 1978

Yellow Horse is the earth Horse. When earth exists in a masculine, yang state, it is symbolized by a hill. If you were born in the year of the yellow Horse, a hill or mountain is your personal symbol.

Yellow Horse benefits greatly by the positive attributes that earth brings to his temperament, qualities that include stability, honesty, practicality, industry, prudence, reliability, kindness, and loyalty (see page 20). Earth traits make yellow Horse unique among Horses because stability, practicality, industry, prudence, and reliability are not natural Horse characteristics.

Yellow Horse possesses a good business sense and can invest wisely. He can successfully complete tasks and will not deliberately contradict authority figures because he is less impetuous than other Horses. The most logical Horse and the only Horse not motivated by whims or passions of the moment, Yellow Horse thinks before he acts and can follow directions.

Fire is Horse's earthly branch (see page 18). Fire nurtures earth because after fire burns ash is created, which makes more earth. This is extremely beneficial to yellow Horse, helping him to grow and find happiness in life. Yellow Horse's prudence, sincerity, and good nature make him liked wherever he goes. Yellow Horse is often valued by loving groups of family and friends. He can be compatible with others because he is not as argumentative as other Horses. He is less blunt and can acquiesce to traditional roles when necessary. Yellow Horse succeeds by demonstrating a sympathetic nature.

Yellow Horse is interested in expanding his circle of knowledge. Like all Horses, yellow Horse learns from travel. Unlike other Horses, yellow Horse prefers to plan vacations with loved ones to share experiences rather than embarking alone on an uncharted journey of discovery.

金
馬 # WHITE HORSE—1930, 1990

White Horse is the metal Horse. When metal expresses masculine yang energy, it is symbolized by a weapon, the personal symbol of anyone born in the year of the white Horse.

Metal qualities—righteousness, independence, strong will, intensity, uprightness, determination, and ability to focus— empower white Horse and make him a very tough warrior (see page 21). One of the strongest signs of the Taoist zodiac, this hardy Horse is physical, athletic, and very sexual.

White Horse has a magnetic personality, is popular, and has a wide circle of friends from all walks of life. He often has many suitors during youth. Like all Horses, white Horse seeks adventure and excitement and wants to do as he pleases.

At work, white Horse creates many ideas and fantasies but rarely completes tasks. White Horse has difficulties negotiating or seeing another's viewpoint. If opposed, white Horse can become aggressive and argumentative. It is not advisable to cross white Horse or try to prohibit his pleasure seeking. He can be devastatingly haughty and cruel to anyone in his way. He disdains routine work, and responds very testily when instructed. White Horse especially dislikes the mundane tasks of housekeeping and child rearing.

Horse is selfish, and metal is selfish, so white Horse is often arrogant and egotistical without realizing it. He can be altruistic, but only when he feels like it.

Fire is Horse's earthly branch (see page 18). Fire melts metal, which can create an antagonistic alchemy. The metal influence can make white Horse stubborn and inflexible. Fire can soften metal's hardness by helping white Horse to develop a more compassionate and less selfish personality.

Balanced metal makes white Horse fair and patient. If positive metal qualities are undeveloped, he cannot make money or take care of himself. This can be a Horse problem, especially if white Horse is irresponsible and doesn't complete projects.

White Horse must develop balance in his metal traits, accept change, and release the past. White Horse's challenge is to tame his self-centeredness and become more sensitive to others.

水 BLACK HORSE—1942, 2002

馬 Black Horse is the water Horse. When it embodies masculine yang energy, water is represented by a wave. If you were born in the year of the black Horse, your personal symbol is a cresting wave.

Water qualities are sensitivity, drive, effectiveness, creativity, and passion for life and sex (see page 22). Most water signs are reserved and timid, but brave black Horse overcomes shyness while being tempered by these yin water characteristics. Black Horse is amusing, clever, and engaging. Strong and powerful, he is lusty and known for his sexual appetite. He has many friends and suitors who enjoy his entertaining company.

Black Horse loves travel and adventure, but rejects fixed plans or an itinerary. Like water, black Horse always wants to be moving and he can be very impetuous and suddenly change course. This inconsistency and abruptness keep others guessing at black Horse's next move. Because he is so lively and fun, his rashness is often forgiven by others.

Black Horse has a fine business sense and a good head for figures. Advancing through his many social and professional contacts, he benefits by planning and investing, not just spontaneously squandering money in the moment.

Fire is Horse's earthly branch (see page 18). Water extinguishes fire. Therefore, black Horse can tone down some of the wilder and unruly rebellious Horse characteristics. Black Horse is the least selfish of all Horses; he enjoys comfort and desires fine material goods, but not at the expense of others.

木 GREEN HORSE—1954, 2014
馬

Green Horse is the wood Horse. When wood expresses masculine yang energy, its color is green and is symbolized by a pine tree, sturdy and upright. If you were born in the year of the green Horse, the pine is your totem.

Many wood qualities—boldness, creativity, idealism, imagination, and competitiveness—are natural Horse characteristics (see page 24). Dynamic green Horse easily achieves goals.

Green Horse is active and loves social events. He enjoys being the center of attention and seeks praise. Green Horse has many eclectic interests. His inquisitive mind is always questioning the state of the world. He is idealistic and wishes to reform existing social and political problems.

Green Horse is unlike other Horses because the wood influence offers some patience, understanding, and the ability to plan. A less rash and impulsive Horse, green Horse is reliable and dependable. At work his fine mind can analyze details. Willing to try new methods, he is often an innovator in his field. He will work hard and not protest when asked to perform. Like all Horses, he loves freedom, but will comply to the needs of the group.

Horse's earthly branch is the element fire (see page 18). Fire added to wood makes a brighter blaze. Therefore, green Horse has a dazzling, intelligent, and powerful personality—a born winner. His sunny, promising, and cheerful ways are a result of the fire and wood alchemy.

Green Horse must temper the tendency to be angry, stubborn, prejudiced, and intensely competitive. Instead, green Horse should strive to be like a pine tree whose branches gently move with the wind. Green Horse must not suppress potentially negative energy, but redirect it.

SHEEP

Key words: Artistic and gentle,
loves the good life.
Sheep correlates to the Western
sign Cancer.

SHEEP LUNAR CALENDAR

1907—February 13 to February 1, 1908 Purple Sheep
1919—February 1 to February 19, 1920 Gold Sheep
1931—February 17 to February 5, 1932 Silver Sheep
1943—February 5 to January 24, 1944 Gray Sheep
1955—January 24 to February 11, 1956 Blue Sheep
1967—February 9 to January 29, 1968 Purple Sheep
1979—January 28 to February 15, 1980 Gold Sheep
1991—February 15 to February 3, 1992 Silver Sheep
2003—February 1 to January 21, 2004 Gray Sheep
2015—February 19 to February 7, 1916 Blue Sheep
2027—February 6 to January 25, 1928 Purple Sheep

SHEEP YEAR

In China, eight is a number of good fortune. Sheep is the eighth earthly branch and symbolizes good fortune, peace, and abundance. There is a Chinese saying, "Three sheep open doors to good fortune." Three Sheep in an extended family were considered extreme good fortune, and three sheep together are a symbol of springtime. The gentle characteristics of Sheep were incorporated as part of Confucian ideology. The lamb kneels before its mother to nurse, as if obeying the correct filial manners of obedience to the parent.

Some translations refer to Sheep as Ram or Goat. This can be misleading. Ram is a yang symbol of masculinity, and Sheep is essentially yin. Ram could be confused with the Western sign of Aries the Ram, and Sheep has little of Aries' fiery combativeness. (Instead, Aries correlates to mighty Dragon.) Goat may evoke the Western sign of Capricorn the Goat, but Sheep rarely possesses the drive and ambition to ascend to the mountaintop like Capricorn, which corresponds to Ox. Sheep correlates to the Western sign Cancer, the sign of the mother and nurturer. In rare instances Sheep is referred to as Deer, due to Sheep's gentle nature.

The year of the Sheep is a time of peace, calm, and contentment. Travel is highlighted as are relaxing vacations. Life's hectic pace is slowed and people are more caring, sensitive, and emotional. Family, close friends, and intimacy are valued. All the arts will flourish and creativity will flow, but such refined beauty and elegance is expensive, and debts may easily accrue. Sheep's love of peace prevents major political upheavals and severe weather changes.

SHEEP PERSONALITY

Sheep is the symbol of love and peace. She is artistic, inspired and creative, and possesses expensive and exquisite tastes. Sheep finds success in all the arts: music, painting, theater, dance, film, design, poetry, and the healing arts. Sheep appreciates beauty and is the connoisseur of all life has to offer.

Kind Sheep is a good listener and is extremely empathetic. She gently helps others to solve their problems and is not critical and fault finding. Yet Sheep rarely asks others to help her solve problems. With a tendency to be introverted, Sheep often resolves issues and problems by contemplating in seclusion. She makes decisions based on accumulated experiences and on her highly developed intuition. Sheep enjoys moments of quiet and isolation because she needs solitary peaceful moments to replenish her soul. Sheep has a predisposition for the monastic life and is often deeply spiritual with a strong interest in metaphysics and the occult.

In the wild, sheep are able to tolerate severe weather conditions and scarcity of food and still survive. A wild sheep has great ability to adapt to different environments and coexist harmoniously with nature. A person born in a Sheep year has similar characteristics. Strong and determined, Sheep perseveres when she must. Often, people incorrectly deduce that Sheep's kindness indicates weakness of character. Sheep is calm in appearance yet strong in determination. Though her perseverance and impeccability are admirable, Sheep must be careful not to let determination turn into stubbornness, and independence into isolation.

The Sheep individual is very sociable. Gentle and graceful, she easily charms people by making them feel special. Sheep adores parties, festivals, and celebrations, and is a welcome addition to any group. Sheep naturally possesses good manners and a sense of diplomacy. The female Sheep is especially full of feminine charm, full of the Tao's yin quality.

In romantic relationships, a Sheep partner is amiable, lovable, and patient, especially female Sheep, who is fortunate in marriage. Very sentimental and caring, Sheep experiences deep emotions. She makes a valued partner, often praised by in-laws, and is willing to help a mate without fighting for power.

Sheep pays much attention to details. She is thorough, responsible, and has little tendency to be superficial. She prefers an uncomplicated, down-to-earth lifestyle and is one who benefits from a simple, yet elegant, vegetarian diet.

Patient Sheep accomplishes goals in life by progressing in small and solid steps, one step at a time. This makes her very practical: Sheep can only move forward! The animal is unable to step backward or sideways.

As Sheep ages, her life becomes better. While Sheep often struggle in youth, in old age Sheep has good things and finds herself surrounded by loving family and friends and comfortable circumstances. This is because all the good deeds that the kind-hearted Sheep does for others return to her. Sheep generously helps everyone, although she may occasionally complain when helping others becomes too demanding.

One negative Sheep trait is a tendency to overindulge in beautiful things. There is a saying "Sheep eat paper," meaning that Sheep spend more than they earn. Sheep don't believe in saving money and would rather overspend on luxury and artifice.

SHEEP RELATIONSHIPS

Sheep with Rat: Both are charming and popular, and have many friends. On a superficial level, they are attracted to each other, but Sheep and Rat are basically incompatible. Sheep spends money freely, and Rat needs to hoard money. Sheep is a good, trusting soul and Rat is a crafty schemer. Rat acts kind; Sheep is kind. When Sheep sees how Rat operates in the world, instead of admiring her, Sheep will be disappointed.

Sheep with Ox: The worst relationship for Sheep is with stern Ox. Sheep is a free spirit who dislikes regulations and routine. Ox will criticize Sheep for what Ox interprets as inconsistency and lack of ambition. Ox works hard, as if plowing the fields. Sheep has no desire to live life as if it were one long straight furrow to be plowed endlessly. Avoid Sheep, who is Ox's opposite.

Sheep with Tiger: Tiger has much to offer Sheep in this combination. Tiger demonstrates to Sheep ways to develop the self-confidence to take risks, be courageous, and undertake new endeavors. But Tiger may find Sheep a bit too weak and sentimental, unless the Sheep was born during the hours of a stronger animal, such as Tiger, Dragon, Serpent, or Monkey.

Sheep with Hare: Diplomatic and engaging Hare is the ideal partner for Sheep. With Hare, Sheep finds another connoisseur of the arts who values peace and harmony, a cultivated soul who appreciates Sheep's kindness and generosity. Both share a love of nature and beauty, and an almost monastic spirituality. They won't fight for power or try to dominate each other. Together they can create a lifelong partnership based on love and happiness.

Sheep with Dragon: Sheep is impressed with Dragon's magnificence, confidence, and power. Dragon is impressed with Sheep's sincere kindness, empathetic nature, and sheer goodness of soul. But peaceful Sheep may find Dragon's intense life too chaotic and unsettling. Dragon cares about achievement, financial reward, and winning in business. Sheep possesses less success-oriented values. A materialistic Dragon prefers a stronger and more competitive partner, but an artistic Dragon appreciates Sheep's finer qualities. Regardless of gender, Dragon will dominate in this combination.

Sheep with Serpent: On a superficial level, both are connoisseurs of the arts who possess fine sensibilities and share exquisite tastes. But they are incompatible and do not share common ideas of how life is to be lived. Sheep spends lavishly and Serpent hoards. Disreputable Serpent keeps secrets and may manipulate to achieve success; gentle Sheep is shocked by such tactics and does not benefit from Serpent's influence. Serpent criticizes Sheep and accuses her of being a naive victim.

Sheep with Horse: Sheep can find much happiness and contentment when moving forward through life with strong Horse at her side. Together they can create an equal partnership. Sunny Horse persuades Sheep to be less pessimistic and to enjoy life.

Horse enjoys Sheep's willingness to understand, forgive, and be flexible with Horse's unpredictable nature. Both are very social and enjoy travel, celebrations, and attending performances. Horse interprets Sheep's possessiveness as true love. Regardless of gender, Horse's dominant personality will direct this relationship.

Sheep with Sheep: Two Sheep are very comfortable together and share a sense of being kindred souls. They appreciate beauty, are kind to animals, possess intuitive abilities, and indulge in the finer things in life. They both strive to please and can find their times together rewarding and mutually satisfying. But they may not accomplish very much and finances must be controlled.

Sheep with Monkey: Sheep is impressed by mercurial Monkey who, like Sheep, enjoys good times, entertainment, and lively conversation. Sheep can offer unsteady Monkey sympathy, kindness, and total attention. Sheep must not allow herself to be taken advantage of. Sweet Sheep lives a less complicated life than wily Monkey, who can be a shrewd and clever manipulator. Sheep's pure-hearted ways differ from Monkey's flexible morality. Yet together they can create a fun, exciting, and stimulating relationship.

Sheep with Phoenix: These two are incompatible. Sheep is a free artistic soul and Phoenix lives by guidelines, rules, and structure. Phoenix may attempt to change Sheep, but Sheep will be miserable if she allows Phoenix to structure her life. Sheep spends money, whereas Phoenix desires to control a fortune. Phoenix's dedicated work ethic is contrary to Sheep's values and sensibilities.

Sheep with Dog: Both are pessimistic worriers who bring out the weakest qualities in each other. Practical Dog criticizes Sheep's caprices and financial indulgences. Dog may attempt to train undisciplined Sheep and insist that Sheep toughen up and become a good soldier like Dog. Sheep will find fault in Dog's relentless need to battle the world and right every wrong. They have little in common.

Sheep with Boar: Boar is one of the best partners for Sheep. Both are kind, gentle, affable souls. Neither wants to control the other and both love peace. Sheep's good heart and sympathetic nature will be appreciated by Boar. Boar's sturdiness and reliability will be a blessing to Sheep. Together they can find happiness and contentment.

SHEEP CHILD AND PARENT

The Sheep child is a perfect angel—quiet, peaceful, gentle, and obedient. She has a marvelous imagination and should be encouraged to pursue the arts, where she will excel. The Sheep child appreciates pampering indulgences, such as scented baths, soft bedding, and beautiful clothing. This child will not bully other children, nor exhibit selfish and cruel behavior. Occasionally the Sheep child, especially a Sheep son, may be bullied by other children. Parents and caregivers should protect the spiritual, pure Sheep child who dislikes teasing, arguing, loud noises, and chaos. The Sheep born in winter has a difficult time making money because that is when Sheep have little greenery to eat.

The Sheep parent is very giving and must take care not to spoil or indulge her children. She is very loving and will provide as well as possible for her offspring, although the responsibilities of child rearing may seem overwhelming at times. Similar rules of compatibility apply as for Sheep relationships: Sheep parent flows harmoniously with Hare, Horse, Sheep, and Boar children, who relish the Sheep parent's creativity and kindness. Sheep parents can do well with Tiger, Dragon, Serpent, and Monkey children, who enjoy the free reign given to them. But Rat, Ox, Dog, and Phoenix children may desire more structure, stability, and routine than Sheep parents usually provide.

SHEEP IN THE TWELVE-BRANCH CYCLE

Sheep in Rat year: Expect a very good year for Sheep in which business improves, debts can be paid, and success is foreseen. Family and home life is stable and calm, and friendships and romances are favored.

Sheep in Ox year: Expect a difficult year for Sheep because Ox is opposite Sheep in the twelve-branch cycle. Sheep cannot create new opportunities and may be stuck performing repetitive and mundane tasks. Finances as well as morale may be low.

Sheep in Tiger year: There will be some exciting and fun times under Tiger's influence. Sheep will be social and travel is foreseen. But not much can be accomplished and energy, as well as finances, may be wasted.

Sheep in Hare year: Expect one of the best years in the twelve-branch cycle. Sheep receives many invitations and attends lovely parties where others enjoy Sheep's company. Sheep will be happy, well loved, and content.

Sheep in Dragon year: Expect a time of stimulation and excitement. Under Dragon's glorious influence, Sheep can find happiness, success, and romance. But care must be taken with finances, and too much activity can lead to illness.

Sheep in Serpent year: Expect a fun year of scandalous gossip, travel, interesting communications, and amusing activities. But all these festivities may be beyond Sheep's budget, giving Sheep too many opportunities to "eat paper."

Sheep in Horse year: Expect an amusing year because Horse is one of Sheep's closest friends. Sheep can be happy, successful, and free of worry under Horse's positive influence.

Sheep in Sheep year: Expect an excellent year when Sheep receives positive attention, has opportunities for a bright future, and circumstances seem lovely. Sheep benefits from the creative and artistic energies of her own year.

Sheep in Monkey year: Expect a good year, but prepare for highs and lows. Avoid becoming swept away by big plans and wild Monkey schemes. Sheep does well to remain calm and neutral.

Sheep in Phoenix year: Expect trying times because Phoenix's influence demands hard work and responsible accounting for how time and money are spent. Sheep dislikes working hard and does best to comply passively, curb spending, and not attract criticism.

Sheep in Dog year: Some problems result from neglect and lack of support from family and coworkers. Difficulties could result if Sheep becomes involved with the problems of others. Sheep does best to remain neutral and avoid rushing in to help those who will not appreciate Sheep's sacrifice.

Sheep in Boar year: This is one of the easiest years of the twelve-branch cycle. Everything Sheep touches can turn to gold. Good fortune is foreseen in romance and business. Sheep could inherit or win money.

火羊 PURPLE SHEEP—1907, 1967, 2027

Purple Sheep is the fire Sheep. When fire expresses feminine yin energy, it is symbolized by the flame of a lamp. If you were born in the year of the purple Sheep, a pure flame is your personal symbol for meditation.

Fire qualities are reason, expressiveness, spirituality, intuition, insight, dynamism, passion, aggressiveness, leadership, and good manners. Fire characteristics add power to purple Sheep and deepen Sheep's natural spirituality. Since a proper sense of etiquette is a classic Sheep trait, expect purple Sheep to be one of the most cordial and well-behaved fire signs of the Taoist zodiac.

The earthly branch of Sheep is the element fire (see page 18). Purple Sheep has a double dose of fire, making purple Sheep more extroverted, aggressive, stronger, and flamboyant than other Sheep. Purple Sheep is secure and brave, and will act on her well-developed intuition. She is rarely rude or crass due to her refined sensibilities.

A born artist, purple Sheep is extremely creative. She has an eye for fashion and a flair for the romantic, and often succeeds as a designer. An exquisite decorator, her home is a lovely showplace. Regardless of finances, purple Sheep will create an inviting environment. But beauty can be costly. All Sheep "eat paper," meaning that Sheep overspend. The dramatic purple Sheep may be the most paper-eating Sheep.

At work purple Sheep is dedicated but tires easily. She is the ideal team worker and cares about others in the group. She expresses emotions and values feelings over logic. In a corporate environment, colleagues may consider her an unusual character. Purple Sheep does better in the arts where others will be less judgmental of her need to feel deeply.

Purple Sheep must temper a tendency toward unrealistic fantasies. Instead of inspiring action, nonsensical dreaming makes her dissatisfied with present life circumstances. When unhappy, purple Sheep can become a critical complainer who bleats about trifles. Fire Sheep must curtail the desire to express all her woes to whomever will listen. At these times, purple Sheep can center herself through quiet meditation.

土 羊 GOLD SHEEP—1919, 1979

Gold Sheep is the earth Sheep. Expressing feminine yin energy, earth is symbolized by a valley, which is where those born in the year of the gold Sheep will be most content.

Lucky gold Sheep embodies the gentle qualities of the Sheep coupled with the good fortune of the golden one. The golden Sheep is guarded, safe, and protected and will always have life's necessities. Extreme good fortune blesses the one born in a gold year.

Stabilizing earth qualities, such as honesty, practicality, industry, prudence, reliability, kindness, and loyalty, add fortitude to Sheep's temperament and give her a sense of direction in life (see page 20). The earth element is associated with the sweet taste, so gold Sheep must not indulge in a diet of pastries.

Fire is Sheep's earthly branch (see page 18). Fire nurtures earth because after fire burns ash is created, which makes more earth. Gold Sheep is greatly aided by this harmonious elemental alchemy. She can easily accomplish life's goals and find peace, happiness, and satisfaction.

Gold Sheep is extremely emotional and sensitive. Allergic to criticism and defensive when questioned, she does best to avoid overly dominant people and competitive situations. Gold Sheep must not allow herself to fall prey to the role of victim.

Gold Sheep is very close to family and friends. Gold Sheep's pure heart tells her to help others, even when it is inconvenient.

Gold Sheep finds happiness in demonstrating a sympathetic nature and sharing selfless kindness. While helping others, gold Sheep must not offer money that she doesn't have. This can be a serious problem for Sheep because the Sheep nature is to be overly generous and to squander money. Another problematic Sheep issue is poor boundaries in relationships. Gold Sheep must realize that others may take advantage of her generosity.

Gold Sheep can work hard and is dedicated. She is serious when necessary and can fulfill her duties. But gold Sheep is rarely required to work hard in life. Peace and harmony are what this tranquil soul thrives on, not power and status in society.

金羊 SILVER SHEEP—1931, 1991

Silver Sheep is the metal Sheep. When metal expresses feminine yin energy, it is symbolized by a kettle. If you were born in the year of the silver Sheep, a kettle or cauldron is your personal symbol.

Metal qualities are righteousness, independence, strong will, intensity, uprightness, determination, and ability to focus (see page 21). Since these metal qualities are not natural Sheep traits, silver Sheep may be the most powerful of all Sheep. She believes in herself and can set firm goals. Silver Sheep desires security, both financial and emotional, and can achieve it through a strong will and determination.

Like all Sheep, silver Sheep is creative and talented in the arts. She adores beauty and will create an amazing home environment. Because her home is so wonderful, silver Sheep possesses little desire to explore unknown environments. She can become nervous and irritated by too much change in her surroundings and is sensitive to the slightest variation in routine.

Sheep's earthly branch is the element fire (see page 18). Fire melts metal, causing difficulty for silver Sheep. In this alchemical combination, silver Sheep's emotional state is challenged. She uses the determination and focus of metal to hide emotions and sensitivity. Silver Sheep's hidden emotions may surface at the most inopportune times, causing jealousy, envy, and the desire to dominate. At these times, silver Sheep must release and transform these irrational and negative emotions. Silver Sheep must temper her ego, forgive herself, and return to the true peaceful Sheep nature.

In personal relationships, silver Sheep desires to please. When frustrated, silver Sheep can be overly controlling of and dependent upon partners. She must allow partners more freedom and allow others to express their feelings, even when their sensibilities differ from silver Sheep's plans.

Silver Sheep is a late bloomer. She often flounders in youth when unable to make money or take care of herself. This is especially true for Sheep born in the cold of winter, when grass is scarce and Sheep are slaughtered for food.

Silver Sheep succeeds by being less opinionated, accepting change, and gracefully releasing the past. Silver Sheep's challenge is to learn how to express emotions, including grief, and find her own way of healing.

水羊 GRAY SHEEP—1943, 2003

Gray Sheep is the water Sheep. When it expresses feminine yin energy, water is represented by a brook. If you were born in the year of the gray Sheep, your personal symbol is a clear brook.

Water is the most yin element, so water softens Sheep in this combination. Water characteristics include sensitivity, drive, effectiveness, creativity, and passion for life and sex (see page 22). Water qualities are extremely compatible with Sheep's gentle and flexible nature. Sheep is especially in agreement with the water qualities of sensitivity, creativity, and the potential to attract.

Delightful gray Sheep is pleasing and compelling. Well loved by the many admirers on whom she depends, gray Sheep creates a special circle of like-minded friends who will take care of her when needed. Gray Sheep appreciates good companions and shares lively times with them. Like all Sheep, she adores parties, fine cuisine, and strong libations.

Gray Sheep easily creates a lovely home environment because she excels in the domestic arts of decorating, cooking, and gardening. Her style of dress will be colorful and beautiful. Sheep "eat paper," and gray Sheep will spend lots of money on fine clothing.

Fire is Sheep's earthly branch (see page 18). Fire is extinguished by water, so gray Sheep is often limited in her ambitions. Rarely is gray Sheep born to be a great leader who contributes to society. Instead, gray Sheep prefers peace, contentment, and the path of least resistance. She possesses the soul of an artist and dabbles in many creative pastimes.

Enjoying the security of staying close to her lovely home, gray Sheep will travel only under the easiest of circumstances and with others' assistance. She dislikes change and at times can be traumatized by it. When faced with challenges, gray Sheep can be frantic or overactive, especially if Sheep was born in the cold of winter, when Sheep must struggle to survive. At these times, gray Sheep must remember her watery nature and flow like a clear brook.

Mild gray Sheep is a sweet, caring soul who tends to be introverted. Gray Sheep's challenge is to overcome shyness, venture into the world, and interact with others.

木羊 BLUE SHEEP—1955, 2015

Blue Sheep is the wood Sheep. When wood expresses feminine yin energy, it is symbolized by the flexible bamboo that bends gently with the winds. If you were born in the year of the blue Sheep, the bamboo is your totem.

Wood qualities—boldness, creativity, idealism, imagination, planning, decision making, steadfastness, benevolence, and competitiveness—add much drive, enthusiasm, and focus to blue Sheep, who easily achieves goals (see page 24). Blue Sheep possesses a clear mind, a creative imagination, and the desire to bring harmony to others. She is a highly prized friend and companion because she is gracious, charming, and generous. Blue Sheep is an empathetic problem solver and many seek her wise and intuitive counsel. She is especially appreciated as a devoted and faithful spouse.

Like most Sheep, blue Sheep can be naive and must be careful that others do not take advantage of her kindness. Blue Sheep sees only the best in others and tries to develop their highest qualities. She may become disillusioned when others do not match her spiritual values and idealistic visions. Others act kindly to gain an advantage, especially Rat. Pure blue Sheep is kind by nature and cannot imagine why others would wear a false mask.

Sheep's earthly branch is the element fire (see page 18). Together wood and fire create a brilliant blaze that helps blue Sheep to express creativity and succeed. Blue Sheep is most adept in the arts where she can both initiate and complete projects. She can succeed on her own terms and does not harm others in the process.

Blue Sheep is very aware of others' wishes and tries to please them. As a coworker, she shows extreme sensitivity to colleagues' emotions. In relationships, blue Sheep makes sacrifices for her partner. She gives a great deal and is very helpful. However, blue Sheep can be stubborn and prejudiced when she should be flexible and open-minded, like a swaying bamboo.

During blue Sheep's youth, she often lacks direction and can become a hapless victim unable to balance her energies. By midlife blue Sheep discovers her power and transforms the lives of many. The challenge for blue Sheep is to release her stubbornness and tendency to play the victim.

MONKEY

*Key words: Quick wit,
        many talents, lack of
        inhibition.
Monkey correlates to the
        Western sign Leo.*

MONKEY LUNAR CALENDAR

1908—February 2 to January 21, 1909   Yellow Monkey
1920—February 20 to February 7, 1921   White Monkey
1932—February 6 to January 25, 1933   Black Monkey
1944—January 25 to February 12, 1945   Green Monkey
1956—February 12 to January 30, 1957   Red Monkey
1968—January 30 to February 16, 1969   Yellow Monkey
1980—February 16 to February 4, 1981   White Monkey
1992—February 4 to January 22, 1993   Black Monkey
2004—January 22 to February 8, 2005   Green Monkey
2016—February 8 to January 27, 2017   Red Monkey
2028—January 26 to February 12, 2029   Yellow Monkey

MONKEY YEAR

Asian folks adore Monkey. The famous Buddhist novel *Xi You Ji*
(*Journey to the West*, also translated as *The Monkey King*) tells of a
magical Monkey who assisted a holy monk on a pilgrimage west-
ward. This story is so popular in China it has been included as one
of the four Books of Wonder in Chinese literature. The story re-

veals the typical positive and negative characteristics of a Monkey individual.

One special magical Monkey, Sun Wukong, was born from a stone. He was born with supernatural abilities and soon was crowned king of the Monkeys. This magical Monkey was smart but overconfident of his tricks. He was so fearless and arrogant that he even challenged Buddha. He bet that Buddha would never be able to catch him. Sun Wukong jumped on a cloud and traveled to a place thousands of miles away. When he came upon a five-peaked mountain, he took a rest. While he happily congratulated himself for outsmarting Buddha, the five mountain peaks suddenly turned into Buddha's five fingers.

To teach this wild, magical Monkey humbleness and selflessness, Buddha requested that Monkey accompany a monk to India to bring the Buddhist sutras (teachings) back to western China. During the journey west, the magical Monkey experienced many adventures, including his fearless battle against the evil bull king, ruler of the underworld, who tried to stop the monk. Due to the events of this journey, the magical Monkey learned to turn his quick wit into wisdom and his rebellious character into leadership skills and courage.

Fabulous Monkey is unlike any other animal of the Taoist zodiac, a fearless hero who is much loved and celebrated. Countless Taoist folktales recall this clever trickster's abilities, and crafty Monkey even found a way into great religious literature. The Ramayana, a Hindu epic, tells of the brave Monkey hero Hanuman, a devotee of Rama (an incarnation of the god Vishnu), whom he fearlessly served in battle. Hanuman is honored all over Asia—in China, southeast Asia, Indonesia, and Thailand.

The year of the Monkey is a time of courage, action, anarchy, and true devotion to even the wildest of schemes. Success can be attained in business, politics, and real estate. Everyone wants to work the shrewdest angle, get the best deal, and win big. Now is the time to start new endeavors, for they are destined to succeed under Monkey's influence. But woe be to the dull or slow witted: Monkey will steal all the peanuts and leave nothing but empty shells.

Monkey Personality

Monkey is ingenious, sharp, alert, extremely talented, entertaining, mercurial, and aggressive. Uninhibited, Monkey rarely gets embarrassed by anything and thus is free to express himself fearlessly in all areas of life. In addition to mental alertness, Monkey possesses physical stamina.

Monkey embodies strong leadership potential and wins trust easily. Insistent on being the leader, Monkey won't allow anyone else to tell him what to do. Monkey is good with his hands and has skill and dexterity with machines. He possesses technical talents and can easily master computers. In short—Monkey can do anything. In Asia, the birthrate skyrockets in Monkey year, as in Dragon year. A male Monkey child is preferred, but a female Monkey is also very strong and succeeds by accepting her yang nature and applying it to achievement in the world.

Monkey is generous and sensitive, and loves to help others. In personal relationships, Monkeys can be romantic and playful, yet they may treat relationships as games and have trouble staying committed for an extended period of time. Impatient Monkey gets bored easily and is constantly looking for excitement, stimulation, and new games. He runs hot and cold in relationships and has a rigid personalized caste system for judging others. Either you are high on Monkey's list and a valued player, or you're not; either you contribute to Monkey's advancement, or you don't.

One of Monkey's potentially negative characteristics is that he becomes self-indulgent in his small accomplishments and forgets the big picture. Having a short attention span can make it difficult for Monkey to successfully complete a task. Monkey tends to skip steps in procedure, thinking he can get away with the easiest solution to any problem. This can lead to creation of a mess that is then left to others to clean up. For Monkey to be successful, farsightedness and vision are vital. When patience is learned, Monkey's natural resourcefulness can help him to become a leader.

Astute Monkey must be aware to not indulge in what Buddhists refer to as "monkey mind": Jump to a branch, peel a banana, take a bite, drop it; jump to the next branch, peel a banana, take a bite, drop it—on and on in a useless cycle. Monkey experiences many flashes of brilliant insight. May he use them wisely and not suffer from monkey-mind tail chasing.

MONKEY RELATIONSHIPS

Monkey with Rat: Monkey is a highly compatible mate with Rat because they both desire success and prosperity. Monkey's resourceful, clever, and conniving qualities are appreciated by sharp Rat, who can use Monkey's skills to further their mutual goals. As a team, Rat can finish what Monkey starts and invest their finances wisely. But they must avoid ego-driven competition, and Monkey may leave if Rat cannot keep him interested.

Monkey with Ox: A close relationship may be difficult due to their very different personalities and values. Free-spirited Monkey is quick, lively, and invents the quickest shortcuts. Hardworking Ox is slow, quiet, and likes to do a job thoroughly. Yet Monkey can respect Ox's honesty and patience while Ox can respect Monkey's knowledge of the ways of the world.

Monkey with Tiger: Tiger may be the worst mate for Monkey. Tiger is too domineering, authoritarian, and possessive for

Monkey, who refuses to bow down to anyone. Tiger wants to be treated like royalty and becomes upset when Monkey refuses to comply. Tiger misunderstands Monkey's motives, and resents Monkey's interference in his plans. Both are very stubborn and a fight for power is to be expected. Avoid Tiger, who is Monkey's opposite.

Monkey with Hare: Monkey is attracted to Hare's kindness and diplomatic nature. Hare is entertained by witty Monkey's fun adventures. They share a love of pleasure. But problems could surface when Monkey realizes that Hare may be too soft a partner to match Monkey in power, stamina, and drive. Monkey may feel less frustration with a partner who is his equal.

Monkey with Dragon: This may be the best combination for Monkey. Mighty Dragon matches Monkey in strength, drive, passion, and stamina. Dragon is impressed by Monkey's mercurial qualities, enthusiasm, and confidence; Monkey appreciates Dragon's boldness, grandiosity, and intelligence. As a team, Monkey's resourcefulness matches Dragon's flare. Success, prosperity, and great love can be attained.

Monkey with Serpent: Monkey is very attracted to alluring Serpent. Sexually, they are very compatible. Monkey succeeds under Serpent's wise guidance and has much to gain from this partnership. Monkey constantly plans new schemes, which Serpent will discuss, ponder, and improve.

Monkey with Horse: Initially, these two inquisitive personalities seem to have much in common. Both are free spirits who love fun adventures and success on their own terms. But Horse lacks Monkey's ambition to win and be number one. Monkey finds Horse too independent to follow Monkey's rules, and Horse cannot trust Monkey. They may part ways due to different goals and values.

Monkey with Sheep: Attracted to Sheep's gentleness, creativity, and charm, Monkey desires Sheep as a partner. But if clever Monkey attempts to direct Sheep's many artistic talents, Monkey must be patient, and patience is not one of Monkey's many virtues. If Monkey accepts Sheep's dependence on him, Monkey can enjoy a dedicated, faithful partner who will serve Monkey. Therefore, Monkey stands to gain a great deal, while Sheep stands to lose unless Monkey is consciously aware of maintaining balanced reciprocity in their relationship.

Monkey with Monkey: The only partner to match Monkey in trickery, humor, brilliance, and daring is another Monkey. Two Monkeys are highly compatible, appreciate and support each other, bring forward their better qualities, and make excellent friends and lovers. If they can avoid the problems of infidelity and competition, this relationship can be one of the most satisfying.

Monkey with Phoenix: Idealistic Phoenix talks about his big plans, which attracts Monkey. Resourceful Monkey talks about his tools for success, which attracts Phoenix. But they may clash before they succeed in attaining their dreams because they are basically incompatible. Monkey likes shortcuts and Phoenix needs to plan every detail. Spontaneous Monkey refuses to be controlled by Phoenix who demands restraint and pragmatism. Monkey will be criticized by Phoenix and does best to seek partnership elsewhere.

Monkey with Dog: Monkey admires Dog's logic and sensible actions. Monkey trusts Dog and appreciates Dog's loyalty in times of adversity. Optimistic Monkey lifts Dog out of depression and inspires Dog to attain goals. But Dog dislikes Monkey's flexible morality and wants to teach Monkey that honesty and integrity can lead to success. Monkey may be challenged while creating a compatible relationship with Dog, and adjustment may be required.

Monkey with Boar: Monkey can enjoy life with sensual, easygoing Boar, who places few demands or expectations on Monkey. Boar finds Monkey amusing and refreshing, and falls madly in love. Sturdy Boar can be Monkey's protector in times of trouble, and Monkey appreciates the unconditional support he receives from Boar. But naive Boar must realize that Monkey is always three steps ahead of the game.

MONKEY CHILD AND PARENT

Little Monkey is a wild child, and his parent maintains sanity by planning numerous amusements to occupy the Monkey child. Outdoor activities and competitive sports are excellent outlets for Monkey child's boundless energy. He may become occupied with science projects, for inquisitive Monkey likes to figure out how things work. He must be taught to share and to not dominate weaker children. Meals must be regulated, for Monkey will eat anything and is content with an erratic diet of candy. Monkeys born during the heat of summer have the greatest potential for success.

The Monkey parent becomes a child when in the company of children, creative and resourceful enough to entertain and stimulate. He makes a wonderful, if a bit inconsistent, parent. Similar rules of compatibility apply as for Monkey relationships: Monkey favors Rat, Hare, Dragon, Sheep, Monkey, Dog, and Boar children, who appreciate their entertaining and lively Monkey parent. But Ox, Tiger, Serpent, Horse, and Phoenix children could create strain for the Monkey parent. Ox, Serpent, and Phoenix children require more structure than erratic Monkey wishes to maintain. Tiger and Horse children may oppose their Monkey parent, and a power struggle could result.

MONKEY IN THE TWELVE-BRANCH CYCLE

Monkey in Rat year: Expect good fortune and opportunities for advancement. Success is indicated in all endeavors, especially with home and family. Romance is highlighted, especially a partnership with Rat.

Monkey in Ox year: There will be some difficulties that will force Monkey to restrain his ambitions. Monkey can avoid Ox's demand for hard work by acting as a go-between, messenger, or liaison.

Monkey in Tiger year: Challenges abound because Tiger is opposite Monkey in the twelve-branch cycle. The spotlight will not be on Monkey this year. It is advantageous to retreat and not initiate new projects.

Monkey in Hare year: Expect a very good year with opportunities to regain power after the difficulties of the previous Tiger year. Hare's harmonious influence helps Monkey to succeed, especially in business.

Monkey in Dragon year: Fun, excitement, and merriment accompany one of the best years of the twelve-branch cycle. But entertainment can be costly, and Monkey should practice some financial restraint.

Monkey in Serpent year: Expect a few opportunities that Monkey can work to his advantage. If faced with emotional difficulties, friends and family can be supportive and nurturing and a source of inspiration.

Monkey in Horse year: Expect trying competitions in which Monkey may not always have the winning edge but can triumph by year's end. This is a time for restraint and diplomacy, which may not be easy for Monkey.

Monkey in Sheep year: Although this is a pleasant and busy year, accomplishments may be delayed due to the actions of others. Time to plot, plan, and keep secrets to be put into action next year.

Monkey in Monkey year: Expect perhaps the best year of the twelve-branch cycle because Monkey benefits greatly by the influence of his own year. An excellent time to start new endeavors, succeed in business, and make drastic progress. Happiness, jubilation, and love will be experienced.

Monkey in Phoenix year: A sobering time follows the ecstasy of the previous Monkey year. Under Phoenix's influence, Monkey must work and pay attention to details. Monkey must avoid overextending himself, which can lead to health problems. It is best to retain a conservative outlook, which is challenging for Monkey.

Monkey in Dog year: Financial difficulties result as Dog's pessimistic attitude can darken Monkey's usually sunny disposition. Monkey's energy may be diminished, and care must be taken with health. Not a time for risks, new endeavors, or wild Monkey schemes.

Monkey in Boar year: Expect some improvement after the difficulties of the past two years. Business advancements, travel, and change of residence are foreseen. Still, Monkey's plans may be thwarted or delayed.

火 RED MONKEY—1956, 2016

猴 Red Monkey is the fire Monkey. When fire expresses masculine yang energy, it is symbolized by burning wood, the creative symbol of those born in the year of the red Monkey.

Fire qualities are reason, expressiveness, spirituality, intuition, insight, dynamism, passion, aggressiveness, leadership, and gentility (see page 18). Creative red Monkey easily integrates fire characteristics into his personality, especially expressiveness, dynamism, and leadership. Unique in the Taoist zodiac, only powerful red Monkey combines passion, daring, and astuteness with high intelligence. Fire gives red Monkey much energy and stamina to pursue even the most unrealistic goals.

In business, red Monkey is very determined and passionate about career achievements and desires to succeed at all costs. He is competitive and wishes to surpass colleagues. Red Monkey will work very hard and is sure of his abilities. His innovative ideas are often appreciated by others. Red Monkey is naturally lucky and sees opportunities where others do not. He is a risk taker who instinctively knows what will and won't succeed.

Metal is Monkey's earthly branch (see page 21). Fire melts metal, which weakens the metal qualities of being focused, upright, righteous, and fluent in speech. Thus, red Monkey can become too scattered. Focus is replaced by gruesome fantasies that suggest the worst possible outcome. Lack of integrity and righteousness results in an amoral unscrupulous Monkey who feels superior to karmic law. Red Monkey is often a poor communicator whose statements sound bossy, angry, loud, and argumentative, without red Monkey realizing it. He can seem self-righteous and self-absorbed, when in reality he is asking for guidance (which is rarely heeded).

Like all Monkeys, red Monkey is talented and gifted in many areas. Red Monkey has little tolerance for weaker people. Quick to judge others, he instantly decides whether or not people can be helpful to him. At times red Monkey can be dismissive to others and paranoid about their motives. Red Monkey is crafty and assumes that others are, too.

In relationships, red Monkey is sexually potent and very passionate. He wants to be in control at all times and can be jealous and vindictive if betrayed. Red Monkey demands complete loyalty, even if he is not always loyal in return. Red Monkey is often unstable in relationships, and must not indulge in neurotic monkey-mind fears.

When feeling insecure, Red Monkey can become coldhearted and stubborn. Red Monkey succeeds by developing warmhearted generosity.

土 YELLOW MONKEY—1908, 1968, 2028
犭侯
Yellow Monkey is the earth Monkey. When earth embodies masculine yang energy, it is represented by a hill. If you were born in the year of the yellow Monkey, a hill or mountain is your personal symbol.

Earth qualities—stability, honesty, practicality, industry, prudence, reliability, kindness, and loyalty—greatly enrich yellow Monkey's character and temper Monkey's negative traits (see page 20). Ironically, Monkey's negative traits are the opposite of earth qualities: instability, impracticality, dishonesty, unreliability, selfishness, disloyalty, and a tendency to exploit others. Yellow Monkey is unique among Monkeys because he possesses Monkey's many gifts and talents but can transform Monkey's innate negative features.

Metal is Monkey's earthly branch (see page 21). This alchemical combination is beneficial to yellow Monkey because metal is extracted from the earth. Yellow Monkey can find the support needed to achieve goals and become financially prosperous.

Yellow Monkey develops communication skills and power

through life experiences. A good student who benefits from education, his intellectual and philosophical nature matures as he ages. Yellow Monkey does well to meditate and contemplate. By doing so, yellow Monkey can heal the racing "monkey mind." It is important for yellow Monkey to nurture himself physically, emotionally, and spiritually.

In relationships, yellow Monkey is a loyal and loving partner. He is the most unselfish of all Monkeys and has no desire to lie and cheat. Yellow Monkey demands much attention from mates, and wants to be admired, praised, and flattered. If partners, friends, and colleagues do not respond in this manner, yellow Monkey may sulk and become incommunicative.

When challenged, yellow Monkey can become flighty, insincere, and dramatic. When balanced, he can be reliable, sincere, and faithful due to the earth influence. Yellow Monkey succeeds by demonstrating sympathy and kindness to others.

金 猴 WHITE MONKEY—1920, 1980

White Monkey is the metal Monkey. When metal expresses masculine yang energy, it is symbolized by a weapon. If you were born in the year of the white Monkey, a weapon is your personal symbol.

Metal qualities are righteousness, independence, strong will, intensity, uprightness, determination, and ability to focus. These qualities empower white Monkey and make him the strongest of all Monkeys. He is a warrior who loves a good fight and relishes victory.

Metal is Monkey's earthly branch (see page 21). White Monkey has a double dose of will, independence, and determination. He desires to accumulate a vast fortune and is driven to succeed in business. Concerned about status, financial security, and the opinions of others, white Monkey does not take risks in business like other Monkeys do. He does best to run his own business. He performs well in more than one job because of the metal ability to focus on a task until completion. White Monkey is a dynamic salesperson, and when all fails, he can be a dynamic con artist.

At times, white Monkey can be self-focused and ruthless in his methods. When challenged, he can be overly aggressive, cold, and hard. When unable to have his way, white Monkey abandons the project and doesn't care about the outcome. Being resourceful, white Monkey can soon find a new project.

In relationships, white Monkey is affectionate, entertaining, and passionate. He is generous and kind—but only to those deemed worthy. Independent white Monkey does not want his partner to be independent and often creates unbalanced relationships of codependence. White Monkey needs to allow partners some independence and not be stubborn, selfish, and controlling.

Balanced metal makes white Monkey fair and patient. If metal is undeveloped, it is difficult to make money or take care of himself. This can be a Monkey problem, especially if white Monkey is a boastful talker and not a doer. White Monkey succeeds by being less self-centered and more flexible. He must also learn to be more expressive and less secretive.

水 BLACK MONKEY—1932, 1992

猴 Black Monkey is the water Monkey. When it expresses masculine yang energy, water is symbolized by a wave. A cresting wave is the totem of those born in the year of the black Monkey.

Yin water qualities—sensitivity, drive, effectiveness, attractiveness, creativity, and passion—help to soften black Monkey, enabling him to be more aware of the feelings of others and to find contentment in life (see page 22). Black Monkey is the most nurturing of all Monkeys. He can easily integrate feminine traits, such as his well-developed intuition, regardless of gender.

Metal is Monkey's earthly branch (see page 21). This benefits black Monkey because metal holds water. Black Monkey is least likely of all Monkeys to allow morbid fears and "monkey mind" instability to affect emotional and spiritual development. Just as metal contains water, black Monkey is able to contain his emotional excesses.

Black Monkey benefits from the psychotherapeutic process and is interested in the inner workings of the personality. He values emotional maturity and spiritual development. Like all Monkeys, he wants to be the center of attention and admired by all, but black Monkey understands this immature need and can temper inappropriate behavior.

At work, innovative black Monkey does well in the healing arts as well as business management. He is cooperative and kind in personal interactions and has the psychological insight to hide the Monkey trait of competitiveness. Still, he is a Monkey and will be successful.

In relationships, black Monkey appreciates his mate, family, and friends. He can work for the common good and enjoys sharing success with others. Yet he is vigilant and aware of reciprocity in relationships and will stop giving to those who do not return favors.

When upset, black Monkey indulges in the mental distractions of "monkey mind." His mind races with all kinds of bizarre, negative fantasies. At these times, black Monkey should ask others for help and not arrogantly shun helping hands.

木猴 GREEN MONKEY—1944, 2004

Green Monkey is the wood Monkey. When wood expresses masculine yang energy, it is symbolized by a pine tree, sturdy and upright. If you were born in the year of the green Monkey, the pine is your tree totem.

Wood qualities include boldness, creativity, idealism, imagination, planning, decisiveness, steadfastness, benevolence, and competitiveness (see page 24). These are strong natural Monkey characteristics (except planning and steadfastness), so green Monkey achieves goals.

Green Monkey's pioneering spirit is inspiring to others. He is very aware of opportunities in the present circumstances and can find the quickest route to success. Green Monkey is a competitive seeker who wishes to improve his status in life. No challenge is too overwhelming in the pursuit of wealth and success.

With his inquisitive and inventive mind, Green Monkey is an intelligent communicator who can swiftly negotiate the best deal. Adorable green Monkey is often very attractive and has a large circle of friends and admirers. He is very entertaining and popular, knows how to flatter, and says the right things when needed.

Metal is Monkey's earthly branch (see page 21). This is problematic because metal cuts wood. Therefore, green Monkey can be his own worse critic, believing the ranting of the negative "monkey mind." He may not fully develop characteristic positive wood qualities until later in life and may lack initiative when harder work is required.

In relationships, green Monkey requires a strong partner on whom he can depend. Restless green Monkey enjoys travel, new opportunities, and all types of entertainment. Green Monkey can be faithful, but only after his partner demonstrates and proves his worth.

When thwarted, green Monkey exhibits a bad temper and is stubborn and prejudiced. Undeveloped wood can make green Monkey unreliable and unrealistic. This can be exacerbated by green Monkey's tendency to talk big but not produce. Balanced wood makes green Monkey flexible and open-minded. Green Monkey's challenge is to control his temper and channel the energy into positive actions.

PHOENIX

Key words: Keen judgment, perceptive, a good planner.
Phoenix correlates to the Western sign Virgo.

PHOENIX LUNAR CALENDAR

1909—January 22 to February 9, 1910   Gold Phoenix
1921—February 8 to January 27, 1922   Silver Phoenix
1933—January 26 to February 13, 1934   Gray Phoenix
1945—February 13 to February 1, 1946   Blue Phoenix
1957—January 31 to February 17, 1958   Purple Phoenix
1969—February 17 to February 5, 1970   Gold Phoenix
1981—February 5 to January 24, 1982   Silver Phoenix
1993—January 23 to February 9, 1994   Gray Phoenix
2005—February 9 to January 28, 2006   Blue Phoenix
2017—January 28 to February 15, 2018   Purple Phoenix
2029—February 13 to February 1, 2030   Gold Phoenix

PHOENIX YEAR

The rare and enticing Phoenix is a universal symbol of transformation, rebirth, and eternity. In Greek mythology the Phoenix rose anew from the flames of purification and was not destroyed. In China, the Phoenix is honored as a symbol of the empress, the earth, and feminine yin energy. The noble Phoenix is partnered with Dragon, a symbol of the emperor, the heavens, and masculine yang energy.

An individual born in the year of the Phoenix has the potential to transform her soul. By overcoming obstacles—trial by fire—she can become a new person. Phoenix has opportunities to remedy actions from past lives and bring this new awareness into future incarnations.

Sometimes Phoenix is translated as Rooster or Chicken (the male referred to as cock and the female referred to as hen). We use the term Phoenix because we find it to be a more spiritual translation with the potential for personal transformation. When the spiritual journey of evolution and transformation is too great for Phoenix to bear, she may revert to the role of a rooster or chicken.

The year of the Phoenix is a time of practical endeavors, conscientiousness, hard work, and discipline. Politically, conservative police states gain power, and law and order are championed.

PHOENIX PERSONALITY

Equipped with keen judgment and a quick wit, Phoenix can usually predict the direction of any situation and act accordingly. Therefore, she is a great planner and schemer. She does not waste time—or money—and is contemptuous of those who do. Because Phoenix is quick and flexible, she can be thrown into any situation on a moment's notice and emerge a winner.

Phoenix takes pride in working hard and following rules. A perfectionist who cares what other people think, she wants to be praised for doing a great job. If this work ethic is taken to the extreme, Phoenix can become overly fussy, critical, and controlling. Phoenix often pursues goals beyond her grasp and becomes disappointed when the task proves beyond her abilities.

A sense of duty and pride characterizes a person born in the year of the Phoenix. She wants to be noticed and is unwilling to be one of the crowd. Her style of speech and way of communicating is unlike those of others. Phoenix's goal is to be different and unique.

Phoenix can appear regal and majestic but sometimes can give the impression of being arrogant and vain. A creative dresser, she loves to make fashion statements and has a great understanding of colors and patterns. Phoenix's plumage always stands out with a touch of personal flavor. Because of her own exquisite taste in clothing, Phoenix may be impatient or aloof with people who don't dress well.

If spiritually inclined, Phoenix can develop prophetic abilities. The highest manifestation of the Phoenix individual is to become like a rare Phoenix, the mystical bird that epitomizes beauty and grace. Just as the Phoenix rose from the ashes to create a new life, the mystically inclined Phoenix individual can overcome all obstacles, creating opportunities for new beginnings. But to become a transformed Phoenix requires development of serenity, calmness, and peace of mind, which are not natural Phoenix traits. The more mundane Phoenix can become obsessive about hoarding money and acquiring material riches, which will not forward Phoenix's soul journey.

Patience and restraint are not Phoenix's strong points. Highly perceptive, she can make judgments too hastily. Phoenix needs to learn to hold back criticisms, especially toward people whom she considers weak and lazy. Phoenix benefits by restraining the desire to dominate others and always be in the right. Until Phoenix transforms these personality quirks, sometimes she can appear arrogant, fussy, and superficial.

In personal relationships, Phoenix is a loyal partner. Regardless of sexual preference, she believes in monogamous unions. One thing Phoenix needs to control, however, is the tendency to criticize loved ones, possibly driving them away.

PHOENIX RELATIONSHIPS

Phoenix with Rat: Phoenix may be attracted to Rat's amorous flirtations. Rat may be attracted to Phoenix's unique style. Both enjoy a lively competition and can succeed with business projects, but soon their competitiveness can become combative rivalry. Over time, Phoenix mistrusts Rat's charm, Rat mistrusts Phoenix's sincerity, and they discover that they are incompatible.

Phoenix with Ox: Ox is an excellent partner for Phoenix, offering stability, faithfulness, and sincerity. Colorful Phoenix brightens Ox's staid existence. Together they enjoy socializing, value hard work and achievement, and possess similar opinions concerning home life and child rearing. In this relationship Phoenix can find both security and happiness.

Phoenix with Tiger: These two personalities do not know how to relate to each other without clashing, and misunderstand even the simplest communication. Lovely Phoenix enjoys the spotlight, but dominant Tiger can outshine even the brightest Phoenix. A struggle for power may result. Phoenix should seek partnership elsewhere.

Phoenix with Hare: Introverted Hare may be the worst mate for extroverted Phoenix. Initially, Hare may be attracted to Phoenix's manner of dress and impeccable manners. But thin-skinned Hare is no match for intense Phoenix. Hare cannot endure any criticism or the tough discipline required to attain Phoenix's high standards. Avoid Hare, who is Phoenix's opposite.

Phoenix with Dragon: Phoenix finds the ideal partner in Dragon. Together they make a great team and Phoenix profits from Dragon's success. Chinese art depicts them in a balanced yin-yang partnership because Dragon is the yang sky and Phoenix is the yin earth. They can enjoy their spiritual balance and find lifelong contentment and prosperity.

Phoenix with Serpent: Sensuous Serpent is an outstanding partner for lively Phoenix. Together they make a beautifully groomed and dressed couple who impress others. Phoenix is interested in Serpent's depth of mind and they can philosophize together for hours. Both value hard work and know how to save money.

Phoenix with Horse: Phoenix enjoys showing off, socializing, traveling, and having fun with Horse, but they have very different values. Horse refuses to settle down or be controlled. Phoenix is vulnerable in this relationship and should seek a reliable commitment with another partner.

Phoenix with Sheep: Phoenix could be attracted to compassionate Sheep's artistic sensibilities. Phoenix may think she has found a latent talent to mold. But diligent Phoenix will discover that free-spirited Sheep dislikes hard work and may lack motivation, unlike Phoenix who thrives on accomplishments and duty. Phoenix becomes impatient, critical, and loses respect for Sheep. Both will be unhappy in this union.

Phoenix with Monkey: Phoenix may be very attracted to Monkey's winning ways, confidence, and aplomb. But Monkey will not tolerate Phoenix's attempts to change Monkey into an honest, hardworking individual like Phoenix. They are too different to succeed as a team. Phoenix does well to forget her infatuation with Monkey and seek a trusting partnership elsewhere.

Phoenix with Phoenix: Most other personalities of the Taoist zodiac are compatible with their own animal sign, but two Phoenixes are incompatible. Together they fight for attention, peck for dominance, and mirror each other's worst petty qualities. Possibly, two female Phoenixes can create a relationship based on the two of them pitted against the world, but even this bond is a strain.

Phoenix with Dog: Both value integrity, honesty, and promptness, but they are incompatible and have little else in common. Phoenix may find Dog stubborn, and Dog's pessimistic world view may be uninspiring to dauntless Phoenix. Altruistic Dog will not tolerate Phoenix's self-centered behavior, nor will Dog obey Phoenix's fussy demands.

Phoenix with Boar: Lovable Boar is kind to Phoenix, who has much to gain from this union. Phoenix appreciates Boar's reliability and diplomacy. Easy-going Boar will tolerate Phoenix's criticism and complaints. Boar respects Phoenix and can learn from Phoenix's diligence. Although Phoenix desires more status with a flashier partner, she does well to pair with Boar.

PHOENIX CHILD AND PARENT

The Phoenix child is inquisitive, talkative, and eccentric. She is a good student, a bookworm, and strives for perfect grades. She appreciates a neat and tidy home and parents or caregivers who provide strict schedules and establish firm rules and boundaries. The Phoenix child must be taught to be less critical and condemning of others, especially younger children. Care must be taken because this child is stubborn and headstrong, and refuses to heed wise counsel.

The Phoenix parent is very authoritarian and allows no nonsense from her children. This demanding adult requires children to obey, achieve high marks in school, follow routine, clean their rooms, and be well groomed and cleanly dressed. Similar rules of compatibility apply as for Phoenix relationships: Phoenix favors Ox, Dragon, Serpent, and Boar children, who appreciate and feel secure with Phoenix's strict timetables and discipline. The Phoenix parent must ease up on Rat, Tiger, Hare, Horse, Sheep, Monkey, Phoenix, and Dog children, who can become overwhelmed by too much control. They require more freedom to play. Special care must be taken with the sensitive Hare child, who may become ill if the Phoenix parent is too demanding.

PHOENIX IN THE TWELVE-BRANCH CYCLE

Phoenix in Rat year: Expect financial difficulties. Phoenix may experience bad business deals, loss of money to friends or

family, and may have to use savings. Others may not be helpful and Phoenix may feel abandoned. A time to be practical
and discrete.

Phoenix in Ox year: Expect a splendid year—Phoenix is happy,
triumphant, and recovers from the previous Rat year difficulties. Phoenix will work hard under Ox's influence, but success
is foreseen.

Phoenix in Tiger year: Expect exciting changes; some disagree-
able and some harmonious. Events may occur so quickly that
Phoenix may lose control. Try to maintain peace amid the new
activities.

Phoenix in Hare year: Expect an opportunity to recover from
the previous excesses of the Tiger year. A defensive attitude
can be most practical in choosing companions, because team-
work is indicated under Hare's influence.

Phoenix in Dragon year: Expect one of the best years of the
twelve-branch cycle. The spotlight shines on Phoenix, success
is guaranteed, rewards are bestowed, and good luck is foreseen. An excellent year for marriage.

Phoenix in Serpent year: Expect an interesting year with some
minor complications. Business success continues from the previous Dragon year, but Phoenix might experience family problems.

Phoenix in Horse year: Although this may be an overwhelming
year with sudden incidents and abrupt changes, Phoenix will
prevail because her security will not be threatened.

Phoenix in Sheep year: Expect a safe year with less stress and
challenges. Others may experience troubles, but Phoenix will
be unaffected if she avoids involvement in others' difficulties.
Travel, rest, and relaxation are foreseen.

Phoenix in Monkey year: Expect a time when courageous and
devoted Phoenix is inspired to put the world in order. But
Monkey's influence can cause unforeseen difficulties, especially
in business. A more sober, practical approach brings success.

Phoenix in Phoenix year: Expect a very good year as Phoenix
benefits by the influence of her own year. Phoenix must work

hard, but affairs are under control, order reigns, and Phoenix rises in glory.

Phoenix in Dog year: Socializing, enjoyment, and good times prevail. Financial difficulties can be circumvented because Dog's influence offers Phoenix the qualities of integrity and honesty.

Phoenix in Boar year: Expect extra work, challenging responsibilities, and minor career setbacks. Dedication to career can relieve a financial slump. A time to be realistic and conservative.

火 鳳 PURPLE PHOENIX—1957, 2017

Purple Phoenix is the fire Phoenix. When fire expresses feminine yin energy, its color is purple and is symbolized by the flame of a lamp. If you were born in the year of the purple Phoenix, a pure flame is your personal symbol for meditation.

Fire qualities are reason, expressiveness, spirituality, intuition, insight, dynamism, passion, aggressiveness, leadership, and a proper sense of etiquette (see page 18). These characteristics add great range of expression to purple Phoenix. Because Phoenix is born in flames, fire traits are helpful to Phoenix's development. She is motivated to accomplish great work.

Purple Phoenix adores the spotlight where she shines beautifully. Uniquely attractive and striking, purple Phoenix is very artistic and appreciates beauty. She finds happiness in the arts and possesses very refined tastes. Intuition leads her to make the correct decisions throughout life without depending on others. Her insights are uncannily accurate and decisive. A clear thinker who benefits from higher education, purple Phoenix can be an outstanding scholar when intellectually challenged.

In business, purple Phoenix desires success, fame, wealth, and status in society. She is intense and competitive when pursuing materialistic goals, yet trustworthy, dependable, professional, and ethical. Purple Phoenix is a gifted financial planner and business innovator who advances more quickly if she works alone since purple Phoenix is independent.

Metal is Phoenix's earthly branch (see page 21). Fire melts metal, which creates an antagonistic alchemy. The metal quality of strong communication skills is weakened. Therefore, purple Phoenix can be a poor communicator. At times she lacks tact and spouts inappropriate statements. This communication style can seem bossy, angry, loud, and argumentative. Purple Phoenix rarely realizes how irascible she sounds to others.

In business and personal relationships, authoritarian purple Phoenix rarely compromises out of fear that she might appear weak to others. When purple Phoenix realizes she is wrong, she must resist the tendency to cause more turmoil and claim negative attention rather than admit defeat.

In relationships, purple Phoenix is temperamental, dramatic, and easily excitable. She has exacting standards and high expectations. When disappointed, she can be critical, nagging, and jealous. She demands to have her way with partners and rarely is satisfied with anything a partner does. Purple Phoenix must learn to transcend these negative emotions through relating kindly and lovingly to others. She must release the urge to control and find fault with trivial matters. Purple Phoenix gains by studying metaphysics and developing spiritual values.

Balanced fire gives purple Phoenix a sense of justice and knowledge of when to stop applying pressure. Purple Phoenix succeeds through warmhearted generosity. Experiences that are fun, joyful, loving, and pleasurable are to be pursued by purple Phoenix.

土 GOLD PHOENIX—1909, 1969, 2029

鳳 Gold Phoenix is the earth Phoenix. When it represents feminine yin aspects, earth is symbolized by a valley. If you were born in the year of the gold Phoenix, a lush valley is where you will be most content.

Extreme good fortune blesses the one born in a gold year, especially the golden Phoenix. Guarded, safe, and protected, gold Phoenix is blessed with both beauty and intelligence.

Earth qualities suit the temperament of Phoenix: stability, honesty, practicality, industry, prudence, reliability, kindness, and loyalty (see page 20). The earth traits of practicality and kindness guarantee that gold Phoenix will find happiness in life. She can bypass many of the negative emotional challenges that other Phoenixes must either transform or endure.

Metal is Phoenix's earthly branch (see page 21). This alchemical combination is beneficial to gold Phoenix because metal is extracted from the earth. Gold Phoenix can find the support she needs from family and friends to achieve goals. Less driven to succeed at all costs, she values friends and family more than prestige and power.

When trying new endeavors, gold Phoenix is often lucky and successful. She is an excellent student, benefits greatly from higher education, and can find success as a career academic or researcher.

Gold Phoenix is the most realistic and patient of all Phoenixes. She becomes very financially prosperous through hard work and dedicated labor. Exacting, analytical, and efficient in her dealings with colleagues, gold Phoenix possesses high scruples, yet can forgive those who do not share similar values. She is well organized, honest, reliable, and valued by associates. Like all Phoenixes, she is very direct in her communications. Gold Phoenix must restrain the tendency to be overly blunt and dogmatic when dealing with others.

In relationships, gold Phoenix is loyal and enjoys a steady routine. She requires a dependable and conscientious mate. Like all Phoenixes, gold Phoenix must not become too critical of partners, who may not be as dedicated, hardworking, and meticulous.

Gold Phoenix must watch the tendency to embrace the superficial. She does well to meditate and contemplate for greater spiritual development. It is important for gold Phoenix to nurture herself physically, emotionally, and spiritually. She must not overwork and become fatigued.

Undeveloped earth can cause insincerity, selfishness, or poor boundaries in relationships. Balanced earth makes gold Phoenix reliable, sincere, and faithful, which are typical outstanding Phoenix qualities.

金
鳳 ## SILVER PHOENIX—1921, 1981

Silver Phoenix is the metal Phoenix. When metal expresses feminine yin energy, it is symbolized by a kettle. If you were born in the year of the silver Phoenix, a kettle or cauldron is your personal symbol.

Metal qualities include righteousness, independence, strong will, intensity, uprightness, determination, and ability to focus. Many of these are natural Phoenix traits, especially righteousness, strong will, and determination. The strongest of all Phoenixes, silver Phoenix is one of the most formidable yin signs of the Taoist zodiac.

Silver Phoenix is a very capable individual who can overcome obstacles and succeed on her own terms. An optimistic reformer, she inspires others by setting a positive example. Silver Phoenix is industrious and applies herself completely to endeavors. Her success is hard won and well deserved.

Metal is Phoenix's earthly branch (see page 21). Silver Phoenix has a double dose of will, independence, and determination. She desires to accumulate a vast fortune and is driven to succeed in business. She is concerned with status, financial security, and maintaining a high reputation. Silver Phoenix must not allow her iron will and focus to become overbearing, unnecessarily aggressive, and argumentative.

Like all Phoenixes, silver Phoenix can be headstrong and dogmatic. She often experiences difficulty compromising and understanding others' viewpoints. She is factual and well informed when communicating but must temper the tendency to unwittingly dominate a conversation. Silver Phoenix must not egotistically debate in order to gain attention but to communicate her intelligent ideas.

In relationships, silver Phoenix is an exacting partner who demands that her mate be impeccably groomed and present a positive profile to others. Silver Phoenix works hard and will share the wealth with a mate but requires much in return and will not support a lazy person. Silver Phoenix can be too controlling of partners, creating an unbalanced relationship. Silver Phoenix must learn to give partners some independence and to not be stubborn and selfish. Balanced metal makes silver Phoenix fair, patient, and less critical.

Silver Phoenix succeeds by being less opinionated, accepting change, and gracefully releasing the past. Her challenge is to learn how to express emotions, including grief, and find her own way of healing.

水鳳 GRAY PHOENIX—1933, 1993

Gray Phoenix is the water Phoenix. When it expresses feminine yin aspects, water is symbolized by a brook. If you were born in the year of the gray Phoenix, your personal symbol is a clear brook.

Water qualities are sensitivity, drive, effectiveness, creativity, and passion for life and sex (see page 22). Phoenix especially values drive, effectiveness, and family. The water trait of sensitivity greatly transforms gray Phoenix's personality. The yin water influence gives gray Phoenix the ability to surrender and change course when obstacles are too difficult and not worth pursuing. She is less critical and dominating than other Phoenixes due to this watery sympathetic nature.

Metal is Phoenix's earthly branch (see page 21). This benefits gray Phoenix because metal holds water. Her endeavors are usually successful, and she can attain prosperity. Gray Phoenix is talented in business, yet is attracted to the arts. She is a gifted writer and excels in the sciences, where her exacting mind and attention to details is creatively applied. She is skilled with computers and all forms of technology.

In relationships, sensual gray Phoenix is a valued partner. She works hard to maintain a beautifully furnished and financially secure home. Gray Phoenix enjoys cultural activities and a lively social life. She is willing to compromise with others and can discuss issues without bullying or shaming. Gray Phoenix prefers to share with companions rather than win at all costs like other Phoenixes.

When overwhelmed, gray Phoenix can be reckless or overactive. At these times, she may need to retreat and gather strength. But gray Phoenix must venture into the world and interact with others to succeed and must not allow fear to prevent her from becoming a creative, active participant in life.

木 鳳 BLUE PHOENIX—1945, 2005

Blue Phoenix is the wood Phoenix. When wood expresses feminine yin energy, it is symbolized by the flexible bamboo, able to bend with the wind. If you were born in the year of the blue Phoenix, the bamboo is your tree totem.

Wood qualities—boldness, creativity, idealism, imagination, planning, decision making, steadfastness, benevolence, and competitiveness—add drive and focus to blue Phoenix (see page 24). She easily achieves goals and is outstanding in business.

Blue Phoenix is socially conscious and has high ideals of how the world can be a better place. She enjoys a wide circle of acquaintances who inspire and share innovative concepts. Blue Phoenix has a creative imagination and is receptive to new ideas and methodologies. She must avoid the tendency to commit to too many projects, some of which may be unrealistic.

Like all Phoenixes, blue Phoenix is honest, dedicated, and takes pride in a job well done. In business she is driven and can work for hours with great stamina. She enjoys a strict routine and expects others to follow the rules. Blue Phoenix will not tolerate colleagues who are unreliable, and personality clashes are likely to develop. The yin wood influence can help blue Phoenix to be flexible with others and to not always insist that she is right and others are inept and wrong.

Metal is Phoenix's earthly branch (see page 21). This can create an antagonistic alchemy because metal cuts wood. Therefore blue Phoenix can be too critical of accomplishments and dissatisfied with life circumstances. Her problems are of blue Phoenix's own making and stem from irrational expectations. She must curb impatience and be less harsh and more forgiving with self and others.

In relationships, blue Phoenix is loyal and sincere. An outstanding provider, she is deeply concerned about financial security. Blue Phoenix possesses the classic Phoenix tendency to make sarcastic comments. She must restrain a sometimes acid tongue and be more generous with loved ones. Blue Phoenix often does not realize how negative, almost cruel, she sounds to others.

Blue Phoenix must transform the inclination to be stubborn and prejudiced. Balanced wood can make blue Phoenix flexible and open-minded. The challenge for blue Phoenix is to learn to reform and redirect anger and negativity.

# Dog

*Key words: Honest, idealistic,
unselfish.
Dog correlates to the Western sign
Libra.*

Dog Lunar Calendar

1910—February 10 to January 29, 1911 White Dog
1922—January 28 to February 15, 1923 Black Dog
1934—February 14 to February 3, 1935 Green Dog
1946—February 2 to January 21, 1947 Red Dog
1958—February 18 to February 7, 1959 Yellow Dog
1970—February 6 to January 26, 1971 White Dog
1982—January 25 to February 12, 1983 Black Dog
1994—February 10 to January 30, 1995 Green Dog
2006—January 29 to February 17, 2007 Red Dog
2018—February 16 to February 4, 2019 Yellow Dog
2030—February 2 to January 22, 1931 White Dog

Dog Year

The dog is a very valued animal in China, famous for exceptional loyalty to family and profound aggressiveness with strangers. These behavioral extremes are viewed as manifestations of the Taoist yin and yang. Dog exhibits yin behavior when faithful and devoted, and yang behavior when a fierce guardian.

The Chinese myth of Tien K'ou, the celestial red (fire) dog who chases away evil spirits, indicates how valued dogs were in traditional China. Taoist monks and Chinese nobles developed many breeds including the mastiff, the oldest breed of dog in the world; the small Pekinese and shih tzu; the sturdy Tibetan terrier and spaniel; and the fierce Chinese shar-pei, the Lhasa apso, and the chow chow. Taoist monks bred chow chows to chase away evil spirits and fulfill the important role as temple and palace guardians. Royalty bred chow chows to protect their property and to hunt.

The year of the Dog is a time of fairness and equality. Controversial issues are given their due, revolutions are successful, politics are liberal, and political oppression is opposed. Integrity and honesty are the values that lead to success under Dog's watchful and just influence.

DOG PERSONALITY

In Chinese society, dogs are the favored domestic animals because they are so loyal to their owners. A person born in the year of the Dog possesses the admirable qualities of loyalty and integrity. Honest and trustworthy, he makes an excellent friend and will always take your side. He won't hesitate to make sacrifices for people and ideas he believes in. Dog has a strong sense of fair play and honors commitments.

Direct and frank, Dog does not pay much attention to superficial social details and has little patience for frivolity. Yet he likes to be spontaneous. Dog is hot-blooded and emotional. He prefers to react to rather than plan for a situation. Only Dog will loyally stand by when others have abandoned a cause. He prefers to live an impeccable life, a life filled with principles and dignity, always willing to be a crusader for a noble ideology.

Dog usually needs direction and guidance in the workplace in order to succeed. In general, he is a better follower than leader and performs outstandingly in team situations. Dog makes a good soldier. He possesses excellent instincts and is willing to work hard to achieve success. Responsible and reliable, Dog inspires confidence in others by being trustworthy and keeping secrets when necessary.

A negative Dog trait is a tendency to be judgmental and extreme. Dog can act as if color-blind, only seeing things in black and white. Others are either friend or foe, good or bad, right or wrong. Dog's intelligence and quick wit enables him to jump to the right conclusion quickly. By applying his keen senses, Dogs can avoid problems.

Dog is very sensitive and compassionate, the type of person who is easily moved to tears during a movie because he is strongly emotional. He especially empathizes with the underdog and is a champion of fairness and equality for all people. Dog can sometimes appear to be loud and thoughtless because he cannot control how he feels. Since Dog's actions are so often driven by emotions rather than reason, Dogs can sometimes plunge into a situation carelessly and thus take unnecessary risks.

When Dog falls in love, Dog falls hard! He is extremely loyal to a partner and would not lightly consider having an affair. Because of this dedication, Dog is usually selective in the beginning stage of dating. Once the right person is found, Dog is ready to devote the rest of his life to this chosen partner. One born in the year of the Dog tends to marry early.

Dog Relationships

Dog with Rat: Both are instinctive and intuitive types who possess keen senses and sharp wits. Dog can benefit from Rat's extroverted nature and large social circle. Both are hard workers who respect the other's independence and privacy. Dog may have to forgive Rat's deviousness and occasional lack of scruples. Rat may have to understand Dog's disinterest in saving money and being frugal. If they make these minor adjustments, they can be happy together.

Dog with Ox: Dog respects Ox's value of loyalty and fair play, especially in business. But Dog may find a relationship with Ox frustrating. Dog may have difficulty respecting Ox's slow methods and invasion of Dog's privacy. This pair may experience communication problems because Dog is faster than Ox

and has little patience for Ox's sometimes dull manner of relating. Ox benefits from this partnership, but Dog may not be as fortunate.

Dog with Tiger: Tiger may be the best partner for Dog. Tiger offers Dog excitement, creativity, and stimulation. Both are dedicated to altruistic, humanitarian concerns. They share similar goals and values, and can communicate clearly. Together they are very compatible, emotionally and physically. Dog has truly met his match in Tiger.

Dog with Hare: Hare can offer Dog peace, serenity, and beauty. Easygoing Hare can work well with practical Dog and as a team they can become very prosperous. They trust and respect each other and they bring out the other's finest traits. They are extremely compatible.

Dog with Dragon: Dog perceives Dragon as an opinionated egotist. Dog refuses to become Dragon's audience. Dog is too practical, cautious, and hardworking for daydreaming Dragon. They have very different outlooks on life, don't trust each other, and do not communicate well. Avoid Dragon, who is Dog's opposite in the twelve-branch cycle.

Dog with Serpent: These two may be suspicious of each other's motives when they first meet, but in time they can learn to compromise. Dog may learn to respect Serpent's introspective wisdom, and Serpent may learn to respect Dog's integrity and selfless attitude. But difficulties may arise because Dog values freedom and emancipation for all, while Serpent values power and success. They may not have enough in common to maintain a lasting bond.

Dog with Horse: Horse is one of the best partners for Dog in the twelve-branch cycle. Horse is perfectly suited to fulfill Dog's ideals. Horse respects Dog's lofty goals, personal integrity, and need to champion the underdog. Horse does not criticize Dog; instead Horse encourages Dog to find happiness through true expression of Dog's noble character. Dog understands impulsive Horse very well and can flow with Horse's direct statements and sudden changes in plans. This relationship can last a lifetime.

Dog with Sheep: Sheep is kind and gentle with Dog, who appreciates Sheep's goodness. But in time they may realize that together they have become pessimistic worriers with negative attitudes. Inspired Dog wants to rush out and right all wrongs, but Sheep has little enthusiasm for direct action. Dog may lose respect for Sheep, who would rather stay home in comfortable surroundings. They may find that they have little in common.

Dog with Monkey: Monkey is entertaining and stimulating to Dog, who enjoys Monkey's witty conversations and funny antics. But Monkey possesses a flexible morality that runs counter to Dog's sense of fairness. If Dog can forgive Monkey his trickster ways, Dog can find happiness with Monkey. Dog offers Monkey the stability and logic he lacks, and together they can become a successful team.

Dog with Phoenix: These two live in different worlds. They do not communicate well, and Dog may interpret Phoenix's words as confrontational criticism. Dog is unable to agree with Phoenix's nonsensical flights of fancy, and Phoenix finds that practical Dog squashes his plans. Altruistic Dog will not tolerate Phoenix's self-centered behavior, nor will Dog obey

Phoenix's fussy demands. They may find their relationship to be very strained most of the time.

Dog with Dog: Two Dogs make a good team. Together they have a great camaraderie, share the qualities of honesty and integrity, and possess an interest in the welfare of others. They respond similarly in most situations and can succeed in business together, but they must avoid the tendency to become pessimistic and too serious when anxious or pressured. If they can cultivate a positive attitude, they truly can enjoy each other's company and companionship.

Dog with Boar: Dog enjoys the companionship of kindly good-hearted Boar. Boar can offer Dog a peaceful home and soothe Dog's anxieties when Dog becomes too pessimistic. Dog's altruistic values are appreciated by Boar, and Dog finds Boar's goodness inspiring. They can work well together with little conflict. Gullible Boar benefits from guardian Dog's vigilance. They will not engage in power struggles and are willing to compromise. Dog can find happiness with Boar.

DOG CHILD AND PARENT

The Dog child is independent, fair, affectionate, and does his best to create harmony in the home and with other siblings. He is protective of other children and acts the role of the oldest, regardless of age, causing the Dog child to mature more quickly than other children. This child can assume responsibilities and become a high achiever. Life is easier for Dogs born in the daytime, because night-born Dogs may be overly vigilant, alert, and unable to relax.

The Dog parent worries about his offspring. He needs to know the child's schedule and can become upset if the child returns home later than expected. Harmony can be maintained if the Dog parent learns to trust and not fear the worst. In the role of caregiver, Dog is superb. The Dog parent relishes parental duties and is very fair in his dealings with children.

Similar rules of compatibility apply as for Dog relationships: Dog favors Tiger, Hare, Horse, Dog, and Boar children who appreciate an intelligent, just, and dedicated parent. Dog is fair with Rat, Serpent, Sheep, and Monkey children, who benefit from Dog's guidance. The Dog parent may have problems with Ox, Dragon, and Phoenix children, who can be very stubborn and temperamental when Dog parent lays down the law.

Dog in the Twelve-Branch Cycle

Dog in Rat year: Expect a positive year with attention on business, but too much focus on work and money can become drudgery and not mentally stimulating enough for Dog. Health is strong and illness can be avoided.

Dog in Ox year: Expect minor problems and upsets. Ox's influence brings conservative politics and restrictions. Radical Dog's revolutionary ideas and altruistic concepts will be challenged.

Dog in Tiger year: Expect an excellent year as the humanitarian political consciousness of Tiger year inspires Dog's devotion to causes. Dog can find happiness and not be as prone to pessimism and negative thinking.

Dog in Hare year: Expect a pleasant year of ease and contentment when Dog can rest and possibly enjoy a vacation. Peaceful Hare's influence makes this an excellent year for Dog to marry.

Dog in Dragon year: Expect difficulties because Dragon is opposite Dog in the twelve-branch cycle. Draconic dramatics and intense emphasis on financial success is uninteresting to Dog. It is best to keep quiet and act cautiously.

Dog in Serpent year: Success is indicated in home and business, as this good year of soul searching leads to satisfying answers. Serpent's influence brings philosophizing, questioning, and debating, which Dog enjoys.

Dog in Horse year: Expect an outstanding year of much progress and success because Horse is one of Dog's closest friends. Dog can experience power in most situations and good luck is foreseen.

Dog in Sheep year: Expect a mixed year; Sheep's influence can offer pleasant social times, relaxing vacations, and beautifying home improvements, but Dog can become very pessimistic and fretful, especially concerning finances. A time to stay balanced and avoid extremes of temperament.

Dog in Monkey year: Expect much activity and involvement. Monkey's influence may inspire Dog to be overly enthusiastic. But projects may not develop as planned and Dog may have to begin anew midyear.

Dog in Phoenix year: The emphasis on material success and achievement runs counter to Dog's values, and difficulties and challenges may result. But Dog could find opportunities for advancement through education or specialized training.

Dog in Dog year: Expect the best year of the twelve-branch cycle. Dog benefits greatly from the influence of his own year. Endeavors are successful, career achievements are attained, and the political climate is perfect for Dog's sensibilities.

Dog in Boar year: Expect a calm and peaceful year. Focus turns to family concerns and friendships. An auspicious time to begin new relationships and expand one's circle of friends.

火狗 RED DOG—1946, 2006

Red Dog is the fire Dog. When fire expresses masculine yang energy, it is symbolized by burning wood. If you were born in the year of the red Dog, burning wood is your personal symbol.

Fire qualities are reason, expressiveness, spirituality, intuition, insight, dynamism, passion, aggressiveness, leadership, and a proper sense of etiquette (see page 18). These creative characteristics add powerful traits to red Dog's personality. He is not shy about self-expression.

Red Dog is extroverted, dramatic, passionate, independent, honest, courageous, and charming. He is very popular and seeks friends from all walks of life. With his inquisitive and rowdy nature, red Dog enjoys travel, adventure, and new experiences.

Metal is Dog's earthly branch (see page 21). Fire melts metal, weakening it. Red Dog often experiences inner conflicts. He wants to be faithful in relationships, but is lusty and desires new conquests. He benefits from guidance but is too rebellious to heed wise counsel or respect elders. Red Dog's communication difficulties stem from a need to talk while being unwilling to listen. When questioned about these character contradictions, red Dog can become belligerent. He must learn to control impulsive rage and apply his formidable energy in creative arenas.

At work, ambitious red Dog applies strong willpower to achieving success. He can work hard and overcome even the most challenging obstacles. Overly optimistic, he will not abandon a project, even if it cannot succeed. Therefore, red Dog should seek guidance from superiors. Direction from others helps him when he is unstable, skittish, or losing focus. Red Dog must curb that fiery temper when dealing with colleagues or else it can surface at the most inopportune moments. Red Dog is fierce when attacked, which coworkers will discover quickly.

Life with red Dog is lively and exciting. A loyal friend and adventurous partner who will sacrifice for loved ones, a sensual lover, and a devoted parent, red Dog still requires a high degree of personal freedom. He wants to do only as he pleases and will not follow dictates. If restrained or controlled, red Dog will become rebellious and sabotage relationships. He easily loses his temper but is quick to apologize.

When balanced, red Dog has a firm sense of justice and can practice restraint; this is the rare Dog who knows when to stop. Red Dog succeeds by learning to control anger, developing warmhearted generosity, and seeking pleasurable experiences.

土狗 Yellow Dog—1958, 2018

Yellow Dog is the earth Dog. A hill represents the masculine, yang energy aspects of earth. If you were born in the year of the yellow Dog, a hill or mountain is your personal symbol.

Stability, honesty, practicality, industry, prudence, reliability, kindness, and loyalty are earth qualities (see page 20). Earth's influence enriches yellow Dog's character and adds needed stability. Yellow Dog is endowed with some of the finest qualities of any sign of the Taoist zodiac. He succeeds in his endeavors and possesses much nobility of character.

Yellow Dog has very strong opinions and is loyal to his values. He is eager to help others, loves children, and enjoys all types of games and entertainment. A champion of the underdog, he can become self-righteous and indignant when witnessing unfair treatment. Yellow Dog's instincts give him a clear sense of right and wrong in human relationships. Yellow Dog—reliable, sincere, and faithful—is dedicated to justice.

Metal is Dog's earthly branch (see page 21). This alchemical combination is beneficial to yellow Dog because metal is extracted from the earth. Yellow Dog can find the support to achieve goals and become financially prosperous. As soon as he wishes for something, yellow Dog has the abilities to attain it. Yellow Dog is lucky and inspires others with integrity and singleness of purpose.

A fighter and survivor, yellow Dog works very hard. He is realistic and can determine which projects are feasible. He works well with others and understands his colleagues' needs and talents. Unlike other Dogs, yellow Dog can think before he acts and makes decisions based on common sense, not impulse.

In relationships, yellow Dog has a few very close friends. Family and friends are important to him. He is kind and generous to those in his intimate circle and shares secrets with only the dearest friend or family member. Yellow Dog communicates well and is concerned about others' feelings. Yellow Dog demands loyalty in relationship and will terminate a partnership if the partner is found lacking.

Yellow Dog does well to meditate and contemplate. It is important for yellow Dog to nurture himself physically, emotionally, and spiritually. Care must be taken with diet because the sweet taste is associated with the element earth. A dog will eat anything, so yellow Dog must not live on a diet of sweets and junk food. Yellow Dog succeeds by demonstrating being sympathetic to others.

金狗 WHITE DOG—1910, 1970, 2030

White Dog is the metal Dog. When metal expresses masculine yang energy, it is symbolized by a weapon, the personal symbol of those born in the year of the white Dog.

Metal characteristics—righteousness, independence, strong will, intensity, uprightness, determination, and the ability to focus—are natural Dog traits. This is why the white Dog is one of the most powerful animals of the Taoist zodiac.

Metal is also Dog's earthly branch (see page 21). White Dog has a double dose of righteousness and will. In Tibetan astrology, the white Dog is referred to as the iron Dog due to such strong metal qualities. White Dog can become a zealot, a human pit bull who refuses to loosen his grip. White Dog is often feared because this iron strength can be applied to either altruistic or destructive pursuits, depending on his disposition and karmic path. White Dog is true to personal morals and convictions, and does not want to be questioned or corrected. This life is one of extremes, with events in either black or white.

In work white Dog is disciplined, strict, honest, and unbending in his principles. He can be ruthless to foes and desires to win at any cost. Money and status are not white Dog's motivating factors; dedication to a great cause is what stimulates him. Once a decision is made, he will not vacillate. Loyal white Dog doesn't abandon the cause.

In relationships, white Dog may appear unfeeling and uncaring. Beneath that false impression is a soul who cares very deeply but is often afraid to show passionate emotions. White Dog fiercely loves those whom he cares about. He makes an outstanding parent but must temper the tendency to be harsh and critical. He has high spousal expectations and seeks parental and societal approval.

White Dog can be self-absorbed, demanding that things be done his way. White Dog does well to allow a partner some independence or this lack of balance may destroy the relationship.

White Dog possesses strong opinions and high moral and political values. He can develop a persecution complex if his ideals differ from societal standards. He is too free-thinking and independent to conform and will not tolerate injustice. White Dog may even insist that others subscribe to his extreme views.

White Dog progresses by being fair, confident, and patient. White Dog succeeds by being less opinionated, accepting change, and gracefully releasing the past. His challenge is to find constructive ways to express emotions, including grief.

水 狗 BLACK DOG—1922, 1982

Black Dog is the water Dog. When it embodies masculine yang energy, water is symbolized by a wave. If you were born in the year of the black Dog, your personal symbol is a cresting wave.

Yin water qualities, including sensitivity, passion, and creativity, soften Dog's tendency to be rigid and add a deeply felt sensitivity to Dog's sense of right and wrong (see page 22). Black Dog is the least judgmental Dog. His watery, empathetic nature understands both sides of a situation. This Dog is the least likely to condemn.

Black Dog is intuitive and caring of others. Calm, generous, and attractive, black Dog is instinctively charming and has a large circle of friends and admirers. He is fair and open-minded, and has good common sense. He can be an insightful counselor, healer, and guide.

Metal is Dog's earthly branch (see page 21). This benefits black Dog because metal holds water. Black Dog can easily achieve goals and find contentment in life. Unlike other Dogs, he does not need to crusade, dominate others, and demand respect.

At work black Dog can acquiesce for the common good and tries to please everyone. The water influence helps him to flow in most situations. Black Dog does not possess the violent temper that other Dogs often exhibit in the workplace. He is liberal and can tolerate much nonsense from colleagues. At times he is too forgiving and may need to be firmer with coworkers. Black Dog should not commit to too many projects or he can become frantic and overactive, especially if black Dog was born at night.

In relationships, black Dog is dedicated and loving. He communicates well and has psychological insight into a partner's difficulties. Black Dog can solve difficult problems and is a dedicated mate and a sensual and passionate lover. When negative, he can be overly indulgent and seek self-gratification, a trait which must be restrained when excessive.

Black Dog must venture into the world and interact with others to succeed. He must not allow shyness or fear to block the fullest expression of creativity. Black Dog's challenge is to overcome fear and become an active participant in life.

木 GREEN DOG—1934, 1994

狗 Green Dog is the wood Dog. When wood expresses masculine yang energy, it is symbolized by a sturdy pine tree. Born in the year of the green Dog, you have the pine as your totem.

Wood qualities—boldness, creativity, idealism, imagination, planning, decision making, steadfastness, benevolence, and competitiveness—are natural Dog characteristics, so green Dog easily achieves goals (see page 24). The go-getter, do-or-die, pioneering spirit of American culture suits green Dog's temperament.

A solid friend who can be relied on in an emergency, green Dog is affectionate, popular, and respected by many. His generosity is rewarded by those who cherish him and appreciate his noble characteristics and love of beauty. Green Dog is intelligent and seeks self-betterment through education and travel. He is a universal ambassador who respects the contributions of people from all walks of life.

Metal is Dog's earthly branch (see page 21). This can be problematic because metal cuts wood. Green Dog can be his own worst critic, allowing negative beliefs to become reality. He worries over trifles and can become too embroiled in situations that are not worth the energy. Green Dog must not indulge in excessive emotional excitement, dislike of self and others, negative judgment, repressed anger, discouragement, and regret. If green Dog can maintain a positive disposition, he can find happiness in life.

In work, green Dog makes alliances with those who can help him succeed. No project is too overwhelming to attempt. He is committed to career goals and objectives. Green Dog possesses common sense and is reasonable with colleagues. Assertive and creative, he prefers to work in a group. Green Dog is not overly materialistic, but he appreciates the fine things in life and wants financial security. He can be eager, impatient, and prone to anger with weaker signs but possesses the dignity to restrain his temper.

In relationships, green Dog is caring and dedicated to the ones he loves. Possessing a communication style that is direct and honest, green Dog expects the same from others. He enjoys a lovely home and desires an attractive partner who brings a fine aesthetic sense to their relationship. Having high expectations, green Dog is not always easy to live with.

When contrary, green Dog can be stubborn and prejudiced. Green Dog's challenge is to redirect this anger into positive actions for the benefit of others.

BOAR

Key words: Peaceful, optimistic, sensitive.
Boar correlates to the Western sign Scorpio.

BOAR LUNAR CALENDAR

1911—January 30 to February 17, 1912 Silver Boar
1923—February 16 to February 4, 1924 Gray Boar
1935—February 4 to January 23, 1936 Blue Boar
1947—January 22 to February 9, 1948 Purple Boar
1959—February 8 to January 27, 1960 Gold Boar
1971—January 27 to February 15, 1972 Silver Boar
1983—February 13 to February 1, 1984 Gray Boar
1995—January 31 to February 18, 1996 Blue Boar
2007—February 18 to February 6, 2008 Purple Boar
2019—February 5 to January 24, 2020 Gold Boar
2031—January 23 to February 10, 2032 Silver Boar

BOAR YEAR

Boar is very intelligent, sensual, and self-indulgent. In China and Japan, the white (metal) Boar is associated with the moon and possesses the courageous qualities of a warrior. In the Chinese Buddhist novel *Xi You Ji (Journey to the West)*, the good-natured Boar character, Zhu Bajie, symbolizes extreme sensual appetite. But Zhu Bajie is well loved and respected because he openly admits to the indulgences that we all enjoy.

Boar often is translated as Pig, a strong animal known for its intelligence. A classic Chinese tale tells of a smart pig who refused to work for the farmer who owned him. All the other animals labored: Ox plowed the field, Cat chased away Rat, Horse pulled a cart, Monkey carried the farmer's son to school on his back, Rooster crowed at dawn and Hen produced eggs, and Dog kept guard. But Pig just ate and slept—and ate and slept. Pig even complained about the quality of his food. Pig realized that he would have food whether or not he worked, so why bother to contribute? When Pig least expected it, the farmer sold him and his life of contentment ended. In this way, smart Pig defeated himself through his own cleverness.

The year of the Boar is a time of self-indulgence and fun. It is also a time of peace, understanding, harmony, and fellowship. Ease and enjoyment of the good life will be valued more than power and status. People can be kinder to each other in everyday interactions and feel little need for competition. Extravagant vacations, sumptuous meals, and lavish spending on luxuries and fine clothing are to be expected. Individuals tend to feel content and satisfied, ignoring the bills that accumulate over a Boar year. The following Rat year will be the time to face realities after Boar year's indulgences.

BOAR PERSONALITY

A person born in a Boar year is kind and honest. She is peaceful in nature and dislikes conflicts and arguments. Boar is optimistic and fun-loving and doesn't hide emotions. Boar makes a great friend, because her capacity for giving and forgiveness knows little bounds. She is generous and trusting and hurries to the aid of people she cares about whenever the need arises. Boar is willing to make self-sacrifices for the people she loves. Good to everyone, Boar even trusts people who are untrustworthy.

Sensitive and caring, Boar goes out of her way to please people and make them feel at home. Boar is greatly concerned with the welfare of others, especially children. She is the type of person who likes to surprise you with little gifts to show you her appreciation. Boar loves creature comforts and desires to share the goodies. Only a few people are allowed to enter Boar's closest circle. If you are one of them, you are very fortunate to have Boar on your side.

Boar is creative and artistic and has exquisite tastes in the arts. Boar pays great attention to hygiene and appearances. Contrary to common misconceptions, Boar is not a slob. She likes to dress neatly and nicely and usually has a flair for fashion.

With important decisions, once Boar sets her mind on something, she won't easily change direction. Boar has a strong sense of responsibility. Once given an assignment, she will carry it out whether or not she finds it exciting. Boar is devoted to her chosen path and career. Often Boar integrates personal interests into her work.

On most issues, Boar believes in the Taoist philosophy that we must acquiesce or surrender to gain peace of mind, as expressed in the Chinese proverb, "Take a step back—the ocean is broad and the sky is vast." Therefore, Boar tends to be noncompetitive and willing to make compromises to allow everyone to win.

Boar can be naive and trusting. Gullible Boar is an easy target for other people to take advantage of. Sensitive Boar can be too easily affected by other people's emotions. She must not fall for sob stories. Gambling and unnecessary risks should be avoided. Boar can be so unsure of her own self-worth that she becomes an approval seeker. Boar can become very upset and depressed if unable to achieve goals. In this way, Boar is a perfectionist.

Common Boar personality flaws include a tendency to be overly sensual and indulgent, especially with food and fine dining. Being artistic, Boar enjoys the finest things and may overspend on luxuries and be impractical about realities.

Both female and male Boars are very family-oriented. They don't like to be alone and will actively look for their "other half." The Boar attitude toward dating is often open and direct and sometimes a little over eager. Once married, Boar strives to maintain a harmonious, lasting family relationship.

BOAR RELATIONSHIPS

Boar with Rat: Boar can create a very close bond with Rat, who quickly recognizes a solid and strong ally in Boar. Rat immediately trusts honest Boar, and has much to gain from Boar's harmonious contribution to Rat's life. Boar will enjoy Rat's charm, social skills, and large circle of creative friends. But Boar must be firm when Rat is unjustly critical, angry or overbearing, or too aggressive about material goals.

Boar with Ox: Both Boar and Ox know the value of hard work and will complete even the most difficult tasks with integrity and fortitude. They can be pleasant and cordial to each other, especially in business, but they have very different values about how life is to be enjoyed. Boar is a sensualist who treasures all the fine things of life. Conservative Ox, who dislikes change, may scold and criticize Boar for indulging her fine tastes.

Boar with Tiger: Boar can find happiness with regal Tiger, who inspires Boar to excel. Boar understands and sympathizes with Tiger's devotion to idealistic humanitarian causes. Tiger appreciates the stability and integrity that Boar brings to their relationship. Tiger will have a grand time sharing all of Boar's sensual treasures and delights. Together they can enjoy life and find happiness.

Boar with Hare: Boar is extremely compatible with Hare, who shares Boar's fine sensibilities and love of the lush life. Both are artistic, creative souls who have an almost telepathic way of relating. Boar offers Hare the security and stability she craves, and Hare offers Boar the refinement and grace that Boar appreciates. Together they find life's magic.

Boar with Dragon: Boar is attracted to Dragon's dazzle and glory, but Boar must be aware that demanding Dragon could take advantage of Boar's innate kindness and generosity. If Dragon appreciates Boar and reciprocity exists in their relationship, Boar can enjoy Dragon's wild experiences. Finances should be watched, since both can be large spenders.

Boar with Serpent: Because Serpent is opposite Boar in the twelve-branch cycle, these two possess opposing worldviews and values. Boar will be misunderstood by sly Serpent. Boar is so honest that Serpent mistakes Boar's integrity for naiveté and stupidity. Boar is thorough, especially with difficult tasks, which Serpent interprets as Boar's being slow and dim-witted. Boar is not the urbane sophisticate that Serpent desires, and Serpent can become venomous when critical.

Boar with Horse: Boar can have fun with Horse, and Horse appreciates Boar's lively nature, but Horse may be a bit too bold and rash for sensible Boar. Temperamental Horse can be selfish, and Boar may experience lack of balance in their relationship. Boar gives, Horse takes, and Boar's needs may not be met—or even acknowledged—in this relationship.

Boar with Sheep: Lovely Sheep may be the best partner for Boar. Both are artistic and creative, love peace and beauty, and share a common aesthetic. Sheep gleefully joins Boar on all her sensual, indulgent, and erotic adventures. The rest of the world can fight for power and status; Sheep and Boar will be happy in the netherworld they create together.

Boar with Monkey: Monkey can enjoy life with sensual, easygoing Boar, who places little demands or expectations on Monkey. Boar finds Monkey amusing and refreshing and falls madly in love. Sturdy Boar can be Monkey's protector in times of trouble, and Monkey appreciates the unconditional support received from Boar. But naive Boar must realize that Monkey is always three steps ahead of the game.

Boar with Phoenix: Boar may experience some difficulties relating to Phoenix due to their different temperaments. Boar is easygoing, forgives all kinds of silliness, and avoids direct confrontations. Phoenix can have a hot temper, is bluntly direct, and can be very critical. But Boar can gain insight from Phoenix's penetrating assessments of situations. Care must be taken because Boar may not experience reciprocity in this relationship. Phoenix assesses that Boar is a giver and may try to use Boar to her advantage.

Boar with Dog: Boar can find a true and loyal companion in vigilant Dog, who will be happy to rescue and protect Boar. They respect each other's finest qualities. Boar can create a lovely domestic environment and offer Dog beauty and peace of mind. Dog's lofty idealism and humanitarian unselfishness is appreciated by Boar, who is also a giving soul. Boar can find happiness with Dog, although spartan Dog may not always understand Boar's indulgences.

Boar with Boar: Two Boars are harmonious together. They enjoy mutual kindness and freely share material objects. These two kindred souls have passions for the finest things and together can enjoy life as one long bacchanal. But for their souls to develop, they may do better with a partner of a different animal sign. Otherwise boredom, stagnation, and inertia could become their pattern.

BOAR CHILD AND PARENT

The Boar child is easy to raise because she is strong, reliable, and independent. The Boar child will do well in school and be a leader of group activities. Expect this child to have a hefty appetite and to be physically husky. Although a Boar child does not require pampering, special gifts, birthday parties, and unexpected new clothes or toys will bring much delight to this usually well-behaved child.

It is best if the Boar child is born in late summer, autumn, or winter because the Boar born in spring will become plump and ready to slaughter for the main meal of the late-winter New Year feast. Therefore spring-born Boars could be life's victims and scape-goats.

The Boar parent enjoys the home, protects and clings to her children, and kindly indulges them. Similar rules of compatibility apply as for Boar relationships: the Boar parent prefers Hare, Sheep, Tiger, and Boar children who appreciate the secure household that Boar prepares for them. They create a deep bond and enjoy a close sense of togetherness. Boar is a good parent for Rat, Dragon, Monkey, Phoenix, and Dog children, who admire Boar's kindness. The Boar parent may experience emotional problems with Ox, Serpent, and Horse children, who possess a stubborn nature and may resent Boar's smothering affections.

Boar in the Twelve-Branch Cycle

Boar in Rat year: Expect a prosperous business year, although there may be minor financial difficulties or delays that could cause worry. Romance is highlighted, social success is foreseen, and Boar has opportunities to enjoy new experiences.

Boar in Ox year: Expect a good and harmonious year in which Boar's efforts are appreciated and there may be opportunities for career advancement, although Boar must adapt to Ox's strong work ethic.

Boar in Tiger year: Expect exciting times—some enthralling, some trying. Under Tiger's influence, Boar will have opportunities for advancement and travel. Overspending and debt should be tempered.

Boar in Hare year: Expect a peaceful and calm year when home and family life are fulfilling, an excellent year to move to a better home or redecorate. A relaxing vacation is very beneficial.

Boar in Dragon year: Expect a fine year with lively social times, much feasting, and celebration. Success is foreseen at work, and Boar enjoys recognition and respect from others.

Boar in Serpent year: Expect some setbacks and romantic difficulties because Serpent is opposite Boar in the twelve-branch cycle. Business may be steady but romance may be unrewarding and complicated.

Boar in Horse year: Expect less turmoil and for romantic problems to ease. Boar can experience an enjoyable year, but care must be taken to not believe the untrustworthy with investments or business risks.

Boar in Sheep year: Expect a very pleasant year of romance, easy finances, and good fortune. Social activities are highlighted, as is returning to school or other advancements in education. An auspicious time for marriage or for solidifying future plans.

Boar in Monkey year: Social affairs and romance continue to be exciting. Beware of financial swindlers and ill-fated investment schemes. A time to guard money carefully.

Boar in Phoenix year: Business rewards and financial prosperity result from Boar's dedicated work if Boar applies herself this year. Patience may be required concerning the problems of others. It is best to be sympathetic, but not become overly involved.

Boar in Dog year: Expect a comfortable year of stability and security. Affairs are in order, although no major advancements or new opportunities are foreseen. Moderation leads to success.

Boar in Boar year: Expect the best year of the twelve-branch cycle. Boar benefits greatly by the energy of her own year. Good fortune is foreseen in romance, family affairs, and business endeavors. Boar could inherit or find money.

火 PURPLE BOAR—1947, 2007

豕者 Purple Boar is the fire Boar. When fire expresses feminine yin energy, it is symbolized by the flame of a lamp. If you were born in the year of the purple Boar, a pure flame is your personal symbol for meditation.

Fire qualities are reason, expressiveness, spirituality, intuition, insight, dynamism, passion, aggressiveness, leadership, and gentility (see page 18). These characteristics add power to purple Boar. Since a proper sense of etiquette is a natural Boar trait, expect purple Boar to be extremely cordial and well behaved for a fire type. Purple Boar's personality is direct—right out front—and she succeeds through warmhearted generosity.

Purple Boar is known for kindness and a compassionate nature. She possesses strong passion and is a creative lover. Purple Boar cares about the opinions of others and tries to do her best. She is determined and capable in endeavors.

Water is Boar's earthly branch (see page 22). Water extinguishes fire. Therefore purple Boar can experience much inner turmoil. Her feelings are intense and powerful, but purple Boar cannot always fully express herself. Her negative emotions include jealousy, frustration, and disappointment in relationships. At times, purple Boar can be overwhelmed by passions and become excessive in her indulgences. When extreme, purple Boar may be attracted to a decadent lifestyle.

At work, purple Boar is aggressive, courageous, and fearless. Boar's blind optimism can lead her to success, but it can also lead her to failure if she does not heed wise counsel from colleagues. She is well organized and plans events with much care. When challenged, purple Boar can be domineering, even violent, if others disagree with her methodologies and beliefs. Her dedication must be tempered in order to relate more harmoniously with coworkers.

In relationships, purple Boar is very emotional and sensual. Her love is true and she will sacrifice for a partner and family. Generous to a fault, she must choose companions wisely. Purple Boar does not always ask for help when actually requiring assistance because she does not want to appear weak to anyone.

At times, purple Boar refuses to listen to reasonable advice, blocks spiritual development, and can be greedy when threatened. To heal this imbalance, purple Boar should pursue experiences that are joyful, loving, and pleasurable.

土豬 GOLD BOAR—1959, 2019

Gold Boar is the earth Boar. Earth, in its feminine yin aspect, is symbolized by a valley. If you were born in the year of the gold Boar, a lush valley is where you will be most content.

Those born in a gold year are guarded, safe, protected, and blessed by good fortune. Gold Boar can find peace, happiness, and contentment in life.

Earth qualities are stability, honesty, practicality, industry, prudence, reliability, kindness, and loyalty (see page 20). Earth traits add fortitude to gold Boar's temperament. She is well loved and respected by family, friends, and colleagues.

Peaceful gold Boar desires to live very well. She loves the earthly pleasures of sex, fine food, and beautiful things. As a parent, gold Boar tends to spoil and indulge children, and forgives all kinds of nonsense.

Boar's earthly branch is the element water (see page 22). Earth blocks water; therefore, gold Boar is slowed down in most endeavors. This can be advantageous to lucky gold Boar because it allows her to think before acting and not create unnecessary grief. She succeeds through patience in all endeavors, and should not attempt overwhelming projects.

At work gold Boar is disciplined and productive and contributes to society. She carries burdens without complaint. She will not quit and will labor to overcome all obstacles. Gold Boar has very high standards for herself, but is not judgmental of others who are lazy. Gold Boar's amazing willpower guarantees success.

In relationships, gold Boar is faithful, devoted, affectionate, kind, and tender. She is appreciated by her partner, who recognizes her pure heart. Gold Boar wants peace and harmony with others. Threatened by change, she can become sick when experiencing too much turmoil.

Gold Boar is generous, wise, and uplifting to others. She can be overly earnest and self-sacrificing and, in an attempt to help, may offer money that she doesn't have. Honest gold Boar must establish firm boundaries in relationships. Otherwise, unscrupulous types may take advantage of her kindness.

The element earth is associated with the sweet taste. Gold Boar must not indulge in a diet of candy and deserts. Balanced earth makes gold Boar reliable, sincere, and faithful. She succeeds by demonstrating a sympathetic nature and showing kindness to others.

金豬 SILVER BOAR—1911, 1971, 2031

Silver Boar is the metal Boar. When metal expresses feminine yin energy, it is symbolized by a kettle. If you were born in the year of the silver Boar, a kettle or cauldron is your personal symbol.

Metal qualities include righteousness, independence, strong will, intensity, uprightness, determination, and ability to focus (see page 21). Since metal qualities are not natural Boar traits, silver Boar may be the strongest of all Boars.

Powerful silver Boar is determined to succeed. She is brave and firm in intentions. When her mind is focused, she will not be swayed from the path. Silver Boar is a hardy warrior who enjoys lively competition. Courageous but reckless, silver Boar must think before acting and resist being too headstrong and impulsive. Like all Boars, silver Boar possesses a sensual appetite and enjoys fine cuisine.

Water is Boar's earthly branch (see page 22). Metal nurtures water, helping silver Boar to succeed and achieve goals. Silver Boar is an extrovert who benefits from helpful friends and colleagues. Proud of her accomplishments, she is willing to work hard to achieve goals and will not quit until a task is completed. Silver Boar endures the most trying circumstances because of characteristic inner strength and fortitude.

Silver Boar is concerned about maintaining a high degree of respect from colleagues. She usually communicates directly and honestly, but at times can lack tact and diplomacy. Silver Boar naively underestimates competitors. She can be intense and overpowering when challenged. When taken advantage of, silver Boar can become angry and sometimes violent.

In relationships, affectionate silver Boar is chivalrous and true. Polite and romantic, she extends herself to others and enjoys the role of rescuer. In some circumstances, silver Boar can create unnecessary drama with its resulting problems. She asks forgiveness, but then may repeat the same destructive pattern. Silver Boar must strive to learn from mistakes and not stubbornly do as she pleases.

Due to the metal influence, silver Boar can contribute to relationships of codependence in which she is the controlling partner. Silver Boar does well to allow partners some independence and to be flexible dealing with others.

Balanced metal makes silver Boar fair and patient. Silver Boar succeeds by being less opinionated, accepting change, and gracefully releasing the past. Silver Boar's challenge is to learn how to express herself more constructively and to heal herself of any unresolved grief.

水 GRAY BOAR—1923, 1983

豬 Gray Boar is the water Boar. When water expresses feminine yin energy, its color is gray and is symbolized by a brook. If you were born in the year of the gray Boar, your personal symbol is a clear brook.

Water qualities include sensitivity, drive, effectiveness, creativity, and passion for life and sex. Yin water qualities are compatible with the gentle Boar nature. Gray Boar's personality is especially in agreement with the water qualities of sensitivity and creativity.

Water is also Boar's earthly branch (see page 22). With a double dose of water qualities, gray Boar is a sweet, sensitive, and kind soul who optimistically sees only the best in everyone. She has great faith that others can overcome all obstacles through correct guidance and nurturing. Gray Boar feels betrayed when other's shortcomings are exposed. She must be cautious that others do not exploit her pure and helpful intentions. When others do take advantage, the water influence helps gray Boar to forgive easily.

In work, resourceful gray Boar is diplomatic, tactful, and empathetic to colleagues' emotions. She is honest and flexible and will adapt for the common good. Gray Boar is an outstanding team player who can bear more than her share of responsibilities.

Gray Boar is a valued partner and a peaceful, affectionate, and passionate lover. Gray Boar is relationship oriented and works hard to maintain close bonds. Sometimes she can be too giving and feel victimized by partners. Like most Boars, gray Boar can be short-tempered and emotional, then remorseful about her uncontrolled behavior.

Gray Boar enjoy parties and a full social life. Like all Boars, she enjoys fine cuisine, liquor, fine luxuries, and all indulgences. Care must be taken that gray Boar does not become extreme in her consumptive behavior. In some instances, gray Boar can be prone to addiction.

Gray Boar must develop a courageous side and strive to be confident. She must venture into the world and interact with others to succeed. Gray Boar must not allow timidity to block the fullest expression of creativity. Her challenge is to overcome fears and become an active participant in life.

木 BLUE BOAR—1935, 1995

豬 Blue Boar is the wood Boar. When wood expresses feminine yin energy, it is represented by the bamboo tree. If you were born in the year of the blue Boar, the flexible bamboo is your creative symbol.

Wood qualities include boldness, creativity, idealism, imagination, decision making, steadfastness, benevolence, and competitiveness (see page 24). These characteristics add much drive and focus to blue Boar who easily achieves goals.

Boar's earthly branch is water (see page 22). This is to blue Boar's advantage because water feeds wood. Blue Boar continues to grow and develop throughout life. Her courage prompts bold action, and her inner strength gives blue Boar the power to overcome all obstacles. She is creative, progressive, and idealistic.

In work, blue Boar is ambitious in corporate proceedings. She desires material gain but is not ruthless in her pursuit. She can finance business deals and properly handle huge sums of money. Blue Boar is a leader who can manage coworkers well. She is a persuasive and eloquent talker who can sway others' opinions. She encourages others to support her ideas as she is supportive of others' contributions and can adapt for the general good. Blue Boar is also gifted in the arts. She is very creative and can succeed in the field of design.

Altruistic blue Boar is charitable, good-hearted, and tries to help others. She may need to be more discriminating with unworthy colleagues who try to swindle her. Blue Boar succeeds in her career because of her sociability and connections with the right people. Blue Boar can start projects with much initiative and excitement but does not always complete projects. She does well to delegate tasks.

In relationship, blue Boar is affectionate and very caring toward others. She loves to entertain and create a friendly atmosphere. A desirable partner, blue Boar is bright, optimistic, and positive. She is very forgiving of a mate's shortcomings. As a parent, she is prone to spoil and indulge children.

Blue Boar may be a late bloomer, weak and unfocused in early life but later growing into her formidable strength. When negative, blue Boar can be stubborn and prejudiced. When balanced, blue Boar is flexible and open-minded. The challenge for blue Boar is to control her anger and channel it into positive actions that benefit all people. Blue Boar must not suppress energy, but redirect it.

The Lunar Calendar
from 1900 to 2020

1900—January 31 to February 18, 1901   White Rat
1901—February 19 to February 7, 1902   Silver Ox
1902—February 8 to January 28, 1903   Black Tiger
1903—January 29 to February 15, 1904   Gray Hare
1904—February 16 to February 3, 1905   Green Dragon
1905—February 4 to January 24, 1906   Blue Serpent
1906—January 25 to February 12, 1907   Red Horse
1907—February 13 to February 1, 1908   Purple Sheep
1908—February 2 to January 21, 1909   Yellow Monkey
1909—January 22 to February 9, 1910   Gold Phoenix
1910—February 10 to January 29, 1911   White Dog
1911—January 30 to February 17, 1912   Silver Boar
1912—February 18 to February 5, 1913   Black Rat
1913—February 6 to January 25, 1914   Gray Ox
1914—January 26 to February 13, 1915   Green Tiger
1915—February 14 to February 2, 1916   Blue Hare
1916—February 3 to January 22, 1917   Red Dragon
1917—January 23 to February 10, 1918   Purple Serpent
1918—February 11 to January 31, 1919   Yellow Horse
1919—February 1 to February 19, 1920   Gold Sheep
1920—February 20 to February 7, 1921   White Monkey
1921—February 8 to January 27, 1922   Silver Phoenix

1922—January 28 to February 15, 1923	Black Dog
1923—February 16 to February 4, 1924	Gray Boar
1924—February 5 to January 24, 1925	Green Rat
1925—January 25 to February 12, 1926	Blue Ox
1926—February 13 to January 1, 1927	Red Tiger
1927—February 2 to January 22, 1928	Purple Hare
1928—January 23 to February 9, 1929	Yellow Dragon
1929—February 10 to January 29, 1930	Gold Serpent
1930—January 30 to February 16, 1931	White Horse
1931—February 17 to February 5, 1932	Silver Sheep
1932—February 6 to January 25, 1933	Black Monkey
1933—January 26 to February 13, 1934	Gray Phoenix
1934—February 14 to February 3, 1935	Green Dog
1935—February 4 to January 23, 1936	Blue Boar
1936—January 24 to February 10, 1937	Red Rat
1937—February 11 to January 30, 1938	Purple Ox
1938—January 31 to February 18, 1939	Yellow Tiger
1939—February 19 to February 7, 1940	Gold Hare
1940—February 8 to January 26, 1941	White Dragon
1941—January 27 to February 14, 1942	Silver Serpent
1942—February 15 to February 4, 1943	Black Horse
1943—February 5 to January 24, 1944	Gray Sheep
1944—January 25 to February 12, 1945	Green Monkey
1945—February 13 to February 1, 1946	Blue Phoenix
1946—February 2 to January 21, 1947	Red Dog
1947—January 22 to February 9, 1948	Purple Boar
1948—February 10 to January 28, 1949	Yellow Rat
1949—January 29 to February 16, 1950	Gold Ox
1950—February 17 to February 5, 1951	White Tiger
1951—February 6 to January 26, 1952	Silver Hare
1952—January 27 to February 13, 1953	Black Dragon
1953—February 14 to February 2, 1954	Gray Serpent
1954—February 3 to January 23, 1955	Green Horse
1955—January 24 to February 11, 1956	Blue Sheep
1956—February 12 to January 30, 1957	Red Monkey

1957—January 31 to February 17, 1958	Purple Phoenix
1958—February 18 to February 7, 1959	Yellow Dog
1959—February 8 to January 27, 1960	Gold Boar
1960—January 28 to February 14, 1961	White Rat
1961—February 15 to February 4, 1962	Silver Ox
1962—February 5 to January 24, 1963	Black Tiger
1963—January 25 to February 12, 1964	Gray Hare
1964—February 13 to February 1, 1965	Green Dragon
1965—February 2 to January 20, 1966	Blue Serpent
1966—January 21 to February 8, 1967	Red Horse
1967—February 9 to January 29, 1968	Purple Sheep
1968—January 30 to February 16, 1969	Yellow Monkey
1969—February 17 to February 5, 1970	Gold Phoenix
1970—February 6 to January 26, 1971	White Dog
1971—January 27 to February 15, 1972	Silver Boar
1972—February 15 to February 1, 1973	Black Rat
1973—February 3 to January 22, 1974	Gray Ox
1974—January 23 to February 10, 1974	Green Tiger
1975—February 11 to January 30, 1976	Blue Hare
1976—January 31 to February 17, 1977	Red Dragon
1977—February 18 to February 6, 1978	Purple Serpent
1978—February 7 to January 27, 1979	Yellow Horse
1979—January 28 to February 15, 1980	Gold Sheep
1980—February 16 to February 4, 1981	White Monkey
1981—February 5 to January 24, 1982	Silver Phoenix
1982—January 25 to February 12, 1983	Black Dog
1983—February 13 to February 1, 1984	Gray Boar
1984—February 2 to February 18, 1985	Green Rat
1985—February 20 to February 8, 1986	Blue Ox
1986—February 9 to January 28, 1987	Red Tiger
1987—January 29 to February 16, 1988	Purple Hare
1988—February 17 to February 15, 1989	Yellow Dragon
1989—February 16 to January 26, 1990	Gold Serpent
1990—January 27 to February 14, 1991	White Horse
1991—February 15 to February 3, 1992	Silver Sheep

1992—February 4 to January 22, 1993	Black Monkey
1993—January 23 to February 9, 1994	Gray Phoenix
1994—February 10 to January 30, 1995	Green Dog
1995—January 31 to February 18, 1996	Blue Boar
1996—February 19 to February 5, 1997	Red Rat
1997—February 7 to January 27, 1998	Purple Ox
1998—January 28 to February 15, 1999	Yellow Tiger
1999—February 16 to February 4, 2000	Gold Hare
2000—February 5 to January 23, 2001	White Dragon
2001—January 24 to February 11, 2002	Silver Serpent
2002—February 12 to January 31, 2003	Black Horse
2003—February 1 to January 21, 2004	Gray Sheep
2004—January 22 to February 8, 2005	Green Monkey
2005—February 9 to January 28, 2006	Blue Phoenix
2006—January 29 to February 17, 2007	Red Dog
2007—February 18 to February 6, 2008	Purple Boar
2008—February 2 to January 25, 2009	Yellow Rat
2009—January 26 to February 13, 2010	Gold Ox
2010—February 14 to February 2, 2011	White Tiger
2011—February 3 to January 22, 2012	Silver Hare
2012—January 23 to February 9, 2013	Black Dragon
2013—February 10 to January 30, 2014	Gray Serpent
2014—January 31 to February 18, 2015	Green Horse
2015—February 19 to February 7, 1916	Blue Sheep
2016—February 8 to January 27, 2017	Red Monkey
2017—January 28 to February 15, 2018	Purple Phoenix
2018—February 16 to February 4, 2019	Yellow Dog
2019—February 5 to January 24, 2020	Gold Boar

Red Rat	1936, 1996	Red Horse	1906, 1966
Yellow Rat	1948, 2008	Yellow Horse	1918, 1978
White Rat	1900, 1960	White Horse	1930, 1990
Black Rat	1912, 1972	Black Horse	1942, 2002
Green Rat	1924, 1984	Green Horse	1954, 2014
Purple Ox	1937, 1997	Purple Sheep	1907, 1967
Gold Ox	1949, 2009	Gold Sheep	1919, 1979
Silver Ox	1901, 1961	Silver Sheep	1931, 1991
Gray Ox	1913, 1973	Gray Sheep	1943, 2003
Blue Ox	1925, 1985	Blue Sheep	1955, 2015
Red Tiger	1926, 1986	Red Monkey	1956, 2016
Yellow Tiger	1938, 1998	Yellow Monkey	1908, 1968
White Tiger	1950, 2010	White Monkey	1920, 1980
Black Tiger	1902, 1962	Black Monkey	1932, 1992
Green Tiger	1914, 1974	Green Monkey	1944, 2004
Purple Hare	1927, 1987	Purple Phoenix	1957, 2017
Gold Hare	1939, 1999	Gold Phoenix	1909, 1969
Silver Hare	1951, 2011	Silver Phoenix	1921, 1981
Gray Hare	1903, 1963	Gray Phoenix	1933, 1993
Blue Hare	1915, 1975	Blue Phoenix	1945, 2005
Red Dragon	1916, 1976	Red Dog	1946, 2006
Yellow Dragon	1928, 1988	Yellow Dog	1958, 2018
White Dragon	1940, 2000	White Dog	1910, 1970
Black Dragon	1952, 2012	Black Dog	1922, 1982
Green Dragon	1904, 1964	Green Dog	1934, 1994
Purple Serpent	1917, 1977	Purple Boar	1947, 2007
Gold Serpent	1929, 1989	Gold Boar	1959, 2019
Silver Serpent	1941, 2001	Silver Boar	1911, 1971
Gray Serpent	1953, 2013	Gray Boar	1923, 1983
Blue Serpent	1905, 1965	Blue Boar	1935, 1995